"I just read your latest book, <u>The Fires of Discontent</u>. I think it's spot on and I want to encourage you in any way I can. God will use this book to fuel the fires of discontent in followers of Christ who see where we're headed as His church and want to do something about it! I will be passing this book around in my men's group at church and encouraging those who can't wait until the next guy finishes reading it to purchase one from your website."

- Caleb Flor

"This is an exceptional book that presents a realistic look at all that is 'new' in America today. It's a troubling picture. But we are not left without recourse to an effective Christian response. In fact, that is precisely what makes this book so valuable. It not only identifies problems, it offers up cures. Every serious believer needs to include this book in their arsenal."

- Dick DiTullio - Some old guy who reads a lot of books.

The
FIRES
of
DISCONTENT

Resisting the Rising Heat of
Unbelief in America

❖

JIM WALTON

THE 3RD CHOICE PUBLISHING

OTHER WORKS
BY JIM WALTON

Assume Crash Position, but Enjoy the Ride:
The Diary of A Middle School Parent
The 3rd Choice Publishing, 2016

Six Rivers: Dominant Themes Watering
the Biblical Landscape
The 3rd Choice Publishing, 2016

Growing A Youth Ministry
The 3rd Choice Publishing, 2016

More Than Blind Faith: Countering the Questions of Our
Culture with Clarity and Reason
The 3rd Choice Publishing, 2016

The Resurrection Really Happened
The 3rd Choice Publishing, 2016

Unimpeded Power: A Study of 2 Timothy
The 3rd Choice Publishing, 2016

Living By the Spirit: A Study of Galatians
The 3rd Choice Publishing, 2016

To my grandmother,
Mildred Walton,
for her example of faith,
courage, and godliness

- JW

ABOUT THE AUTHOR

Jim Walton is a career youth pastor, having served on church staff in that capacity for 35 years. In addition to serving as youth pastor, as is common on many church staffs he also served as Director of Christian Education, Choir Director, Assistant Pastor, interim pastor, Worship Leader, and Pastor of Family Ministries.

Jim got his B.A. degree (with honors) in Christian Education from Wheaton College, and an M.A. (with honors) in Christian Ministry from Wheaton Graduate School. He has written nine books, has been published dozens of times in magazines and journals, and has given seminars at the national level (Youth Specialties National Youth Workers Convention), at colleges, many New York State Sunday School Conventions, Iron Sharpens Iron Men's Conferences, churches, events, and he participates in discussion forums. He has spoken at more than 100 retreats, has led both domestic and foreign missions trips, and has trained pastors in the United States and abroad.

He is currently the founder and director of "The 3rd Choice" (www.the3rdchoice.org), an evangelistic, apologetics, and discipling online ministry—reclaiming people with the truth of Christ. The 3rd Choice's goal is to use the Internet to reach out to the people who want to dialogue, whether you are a Christian or skeptic, professor or student, scientist, atheist, doubter or disciple. The website presents a safe and anonymous Internet environment to dialogue about spiritual topics. He also trains churches to understand the changes needed to keep people in the faith, providing resources for Christians through speaking, Bible commentary and training workshops.

CONTENTS

INTRODUCTION

The Church has competition. The Center for Inquiry, the world headquarters for secular humanism, holds strategy sessions to help atheism progress and flourish in America as well as globally. Some of their strategies are as follows:

1. Create doubt in the minds of kids (CFI[1] has started "Camp Inquiry" for children to indoctrinate them in atheism; they have started college campus groups, similar to those of parachurch organizations).
2. Divide the Church by whatever means possible and necessary.
3. Use the judiciary to marginalize Christian faith.
4. Stage rallies (such as the "Reason Rally") portraying atheism as the thinking person's choice and Christianity as the idiot's fantasy world.

While the Devil is busy in his workshop and actively planning the downfall of religion, what is the Church doing?

1. We are reducing educational settings such as Sunday School. Most churches now have strategies that are limited to worship services, life groups, church planting efforts, and some community outreach. The preaching is the primary teaching time, and all other ministries are secondary to it.
2. We take our students on short-term mission trips, but we are not training them to be missionaries.

---

[1] Center for Inquiry, Buffalo NY

3. We are fighting worship wars.
4. We have youth groups, but are not training our students in doctrine or apologetics.
5. Pastors act like they are in competition with other pastors for attendees.
6. We are not having strategy sessions.
7. Christians are generally afraid of both evangelism and one-to-one discipleship.
8. We are using value-based biblical curriculum in our children's departments, but are not training them in the Word of God.
9. Not many Christians know what to do with what they have learned.

As a consequence, our student and young adult populations can hardly climb over each other fast enough to get out the back door of the church and, unlike previous years, many are not coming back after they sow their wild oats in college. They are being persuaded that the Bible is full of errors and that Christianity is unfounded.

This book reveals ten overarching paradigms in our culture and how they all manifest in subtle ways a falling away from a Christian foundation. The slope downwards is so gentle and nonchalant that our society is becoming secular a whisper at a time.

You have no doubt heard the story that if you put a frog in a pot of water, he will sit there contentedly. And if you bring up the heat gradually, the frog will not even be aware of his changing body temperature to match the water temperature, and will not try to escape. In time, the frog will die, peacefully and unsuspectingly, because he never felt the urge to get out of the heat and he boils to death.

Instead of following the culture blindly, the Church needs to wake up, to become aware of the gentle but slippery slope (the rising heat), to get off the cultural conveyor belt, change directions, and learn how best to speak cross-culturally to our own neighbors, because their language and ours are no longer the same. The fires of discontent are raging, and if the Church doesn't act radically and soon, we may find ourselves boiling with them, without ever crying for help or blowing a whistle of warning, let alone doing much of anything about it except tending to our own flocks.

We no longer live in a society with a Christian foundation. Our proper response to not to complain, but to train; not to close in, but to reach out; not to give up because the world is hopeless, but to stand up and make disciples.

I

||||||||||||||||||||||||||||||||||||||||||||||||||||||||||||||||||||||||||||||||

THE PROLIFERATION OF PARADIGMS

Every word and action has a context, and contexts decide meanings. The same word spoken by one person at home today can be perceived totally differently spoken by another person at work tomorrow in a different context. After forty years together, my wife and I even have a context in our communication, as do all families, couples, and siblings. Words, gestures and expressions are all heard as a link in a chain, with meaning attached like baggage, and not as isolated utterances.

Cultures also have contexts. Persons within the culture catch the clues. In 2014 I spent two weeks in Bangladesh. Culturally I was like a fish out of water—I have no shared experiences with them and am unfamiliar with their cultural clues and shared experiences as Bangladeshis. In America, I recognize the cultural clues, the body language, and the common experiences we share as a culture: Football, knowledge about Reaganomics, 9-1-1, Monica Lewinsky, Rube Goldberg, shopping malls, Einstein, pluralism, fast food, and the Beatles. These are not only cultural markers and signs, but definitive reference points that become paradigms.

A cultural paradigm is "a constellation of 'values, principles, attitudes, beliefs, and myths' by which a society finds value and meaning, both individually and creatively."[2] These paradigms become our cultural DNA, our "American Way," our identity as a people together. They form the skeletal framework of our society, and subconsciously we live as naturally by these paradigms as we breathe and sleep. For us, it's "life as usual."

In The Structure of Scientific Revolutions,[3] Thomas Kuhn writes that paradigms are not just cultural points of interest, but they are a set of rules that establish boundaries and define success. In other words, to break the paradigm is to invite ruin. That's not to say paradigms never change, for they do, but only slowly and with great cultural disequilibrium. A society resists new paradigms, and there are a great many casualties in the process.

Modern societies are going through one major and obvious paradigm change right now, and that is the shift from written to digital information. It is putting book publishers, newspapers, recording companies, magazines, and even some libraries out of business, while adapters like Google and Apple are posting record profits. Cars are changing from mechanical machines to computerized hybrids and even self-driving wonders. Long ago film gave way to digital cameras. We now shop, bank, communicate, digest media, and educate digitally. For each of us who carries a smart phone, we hold in hands access to all the information the world has ever

---

[2] Margaret Somerville, McGill University law professor
[3] Thomas S. Kuhn, University of Chicago Press, 3rd Edition 1996

known and the capability to talk to any individual on the planet instantly.

Paradigms Are Filters

Our cultural paradigms color the way we interpret information, and they also filter incoming experiences. We are constantly and inevitably viewing the world through our paradigms. Think about the instantaneity of current society compared to the one in which the Baby Boomers grew up. Today's generation doesn't know the slower world of typewriters, dial phones, ditto machines, getting up to change the channel on TV, antennas, and film cameras. They have computers, email, speed dial, microwaves, remotes, smart phones, and Kindle. The digital paradigm is how they both filter incoming experiences and how they interpret information. All paradigm changes come at a price, however.

In business, there is a crucial and profound truth hiding behind all paradigm changes: the "going back to zero" rule—when a paradigm shifts, everyone goes back to zero.[4] Everyone. Past success guarantees nothing for the present or the future, for all the rules have changed, the steps to success have changed, and the way we evaluate our progress has to be rewritten. We learned how to use computers, but now we have to learn how to use smart phones. We learned how to use a VHS player, but then DVDs, Netflix, Roku, and the cloud. We have to learn how to access our medical records online, help our kids with their homework online, and shop online. Prospective couples are even learning how to date online. Every change means we have to learn all over again from the start how to navigate the brave new world.

---

[4] Joel Arthur Barker, "Discovering the Future: The Business of Paradigms," 1986, video series

Decades ago Alvin Toffler wrote Future Shock[5] and John Naisbitt wrote Megatrends.[6] Both of these works were instrumental in revealing paradigmatic changes to a culture in flux. One of the points that came out in these books is that change would be the new normal and that it would accelerate dramatically as the digital era invaded all of life. We have seen and experienced the truth of their prescience. Paradigm changes are now an accepted though disquieting part of "life as usual." Over and over again we all have to go back to the starting line to learn a new skill, a new way of accomplishing normal tasks, or a new way to look at things. We love it, and we hate it. We can see the benefits, but we sometimes long for simpler days. The new paradigms have become our way of life.

The gospel is no different. It is never heard in isolation, but always against the background of the cultural milieu in which one lives."[7] Americans read the Bible differently than those who lived a century ago did. We read the Bible differently than Middle Easterners, differently than Africans, and differently than the Japanese. Believers read the Bible differently than atheists. Men read the Bible differently than women. While we try to be as objective as possible, we are irrefutably and hopelessly bound by our culture, our era, our educations, enculturations, experiences, and even our personalities. It doesn't mean we read the Bible wrongly, but only that we can't help but read it contextually. An examination of the paradigms of our present culture will help us to understand not only unbelief in America,

---

[5] Alvin Toffler, Future Shock (Toronto, Canada: Bantam Books, 1970)

[6] John Naisbitt, Megatrends: Ten New Direction Transforming Our Lives (New York, NY: Warner Books, 1982)

[7] William Lane Craig, "Faith, Reason and the Necessity of Apologetics," To Everyone An Answer: A Case for the Christian Worldview, edited by Francis J. Beckwith, William Lane Craig, and J.P. Moreland (Downers Grove, IL: IVP Academic, a division of InterVarsity Press, 2004) p. 22

but how best to communicate the gospel in a society of raging discontent.

The Raging Discontent

What is the raging discontent? It is unbelief in God. The people who claim no religious affiliations (the "nones") are the fastest growing religious demographic in America. The number of people who have "deconverted" (left Christianity and renounced it as their faith) is on the rapid rise and accelerating. The Christian community is struggling to remain connected with the next generation of teens and young adults.[8] Depending on which report you read, statistics say that anywhere from 70-88% of churched youth walk away from the church during their college years.[9] By the middle of their sophomore year, more than three-quarters of religious teens are no longer "churched." That's an attrition rate that no business could ever sustain. One out of five adults (23%) and 1 out of 3 young adults under age 20 now consider themselves "religiously unaffiliated."[10] Ken Ham's America's Research Group says that "95% of 20- to 29-year-old evangelicals attend church regularly during their elementary and middle school years. Only 55% continued to attend to the end of high school. By the end of college, only 11% were still attending church. The next generation of believers is draining from the churches." In other words, we are quickly and unmistakably losing a whole generation. For God's sake, this clamorous urgency to escape Christianity needs to be reversed. The Church needs to change its own paradigm to continue to pursue the Great Commission. While the raging fires of discontent is a

---

[8] George Barna

[9] Youth Transition Network, George Barna

[10] Pew Forum on Religion and Public Life, 2012

recent phenomenon, it is generational and is resulting in a mass exodus—an "anti-revival"— from the church by the newly and happily deconverted.

In the following chapters I will explore ten paradigms that not only define our culture but also speak to our religious temperature. In the same way that art mimics life, so also the conditions of our culture, such as the drift away from a biblical foundation, help to create the paradigms that define us. The fires of discontent are all around us, and among us. How we handle them will chart the course for the future of our faith and life. As Naisbitt said, "The most reliable way to anticipate the future is by understanding the present."[11]

Discussion Questions

1. Do you understand "paradigms" enough to explain it to someone else? Share around the room your understandings of what a paradigm is so that the breadth and depth of it is understood by all before you move on.
2. What are some examples of paradigms in the business world? In the church?
3. How do paradigms affect how we think and live?
4. Why is understanding paradigms helpful to us?

---

[11] John Naisbitt, Megatrends: Ten New Directions Transforming Our Lives (New York, NY: Warner Books, 1982) p. xxiii

2

||||||||||||||||||||||||||||||||||||||||||||||||||||||||||||||||||||||||||||||||||||||||||||||

SCIENTIFIC EVIDENCE: THE NEW RELIGION

Most of us work really hard not to be idiots. And we hate to get caught being gullible because we know we live in a shame/shame culture: we'll put you down if you're successful (while we pretend to celebrate you), and we'll put you down if you're not successful. It creates an environment of insecurity and a culture of criticism, and the result is that one of the worst fears we carry with us is the fear of devotedly following a cause or a proposition that turns out to be false. In that case we're both gullible and stupid, and our friends (or "frenemies") never let us forget it.

In addition, we live in an era where the wondrous discoveries of science give us almost daily gasps. Advances in medicine allow us to do things that were barely the fantasies of science fiction even twenty years ago. The computer has turbocharged our culture, with knowledge and technical capabilities outstripping any human capcity to keep up with either of them, let alone all of them. There is so much information available that the best

Google can do is "1,720,000,000 results (.044 seconds)." Good luck with that one. We are able to gaze at stars being formed at the edges (maybe?) of the universe as well as at microparticles colliding with each other in nanospace. We now know the cell to be a veritable miraculous machine of intricacy and efficiency. We can conduct war through unmanned drones from the safety of a control room thousands of miles away. We can hold peace conferences across the globe on our smartphones. The progress of science has blitzkrieged our sense of comprehension and overloaded all of our neural circuits with amazement.

If we put these two cultural components together, we arrive at one of the most prominent governing paradigms of our time. Most clearly put, it's "Prove it to me." Truth is no longer in experience, intuitions, observations, reason, and metaphysics, but in evidence. Science has become, in a very real sense, the major religion of our time, purporting to tell us who we are, how we got here, what our purpose is, where we are going, and everything there is to know about these subjects. Science is now looked upon by some as the source of information even of "Is there a God?", "Are miracles possible?", and "What is the purpose of life?"

On top of that, the assumptions of the paradigm are decidedly negative: It doesn't exist if you can't prove it. It didn't happen if you can't prove it. The negative (it's impossible) is assumed until controlled, laboratorial scientific evidence can be given to pull something into the positive "truth" category.

God Doesn't Fit the Scientific Model

With those criteria for knowledge and truth, God doesn't stand a chance. "We assume he doesn't exist unless you can give us verifiable scientific proof that He does," atheists have said to me. Since such proof cannot be given, tested in a controlled environment, and scientifically verified by peer review, therefore "God does not exist."

Scripture is also presupposed to be false because we have no scientific corroboration of what is claimed. God doesn't exist, it is assumed, since he cannot be proved by the only evidence atheists will accept. But if God did exist, all of his actions must be also verifiable by scientific tests. Furthermore, if God does exist, he is eternally guilty, immoral, flawed, and cruel, because that's what the supposed evidence shows: He kills innocent people, slaughters babies and butchers animals. He set up Adam and Eve, punished them for falling for the trick, and barbarically sends most of humanity to hell for failure to stroke his ego, and acts on earth like a spoiled, self-centered child. In one conversation I had, this paradigm of scientific positivism (only scientific proof counts) was expressed this way:

> Religions very much seem to be superfluous institutions built on flimsy evidence and wishful thinking, and sometimes deliberate manipulation. Yet what's worse is that in spite of absent or contradictory evidence, people go on about its absolute, inescapable truth.
>
> I don't understand why people believe these things. Surely everyone has seriously doubted that a 1st century preacher and carpenter was truly the son of God. That he was God. And that he can vouch for us morally. That we need a moral voucher at all. Right? God never directly speaks or appears, why do people still believe in him? Why do they think he's a part of the real world, outside of our imaginations? Why have people ever thought that?

I'm having a hard time grasping this. Because now my family is mistaken, most of the world is mistaken, I have been mistaken. And I'll be looked down on if I say that I think we are. All of humanity seems to be sorely misguided, and I don't understand why more people aren't aware or concerned about this. From the outside it all looks so fake. It's a magnificent fantasy, and everyone's so content to live in it, ultimately because it makes them feel better about dying. Just because it feels better, though, doesn't mean it's true. Yet communities reinforce the feeling anyway. And this kind of makes me mad. Also really sad. Disappointed. Maybe a little afraid.

I've spent so much time in recent months trying to understand why religion is still so stubbornly here, but I don't. The truth will set you free, we are told, but it hardly feels that way. And I don't know what to do.[12]

There is no sense of the transcendent or the metaphysical, but only of the concrete and empirical. Our televisions are replete with a new genre of detective shows (NCIS and its offshoots, Criminal Minds and its offshoots) as well as medical shows (Grey's Anatomy, Chicago Med, Code Black, Rosewood, and a half a dozen others). They all push the same paradigm: if you can't prove it by science, it isn't true. Agent DiNozzo on NCIS summarized it well when he said, "What are the facts? We don't assume, we verify."[13]

---

[12] Hoyepolloi, on reddit

[13] Agent DiNozzo, on NCIS, May 17, 2016

One person said to me, "I'm all for spreading love and good will. I'm as hippy as they come. I'm just not OK with basing hope and promise in an asinine notion of fairy tales when there are real, fact-based answers and solutions to be found. You can sit in the woods and pray for a god to drop a dead fish in your lap, or you can walk to the sea and get your own fish. Feel free to wish, hope, and pray in one hand, then sh** in the other. Please report back and tell me which one filled up first."

Atheists readily accuse Christians of "blind faith," (by which they mean "idiotic gullibility"), and assert that "there is no evidence for anything Christians believe." I have been told "Every Christian is intellectually dishonest" and "Christians are ignorant; they don't have the sense God gave a screwdriver. They believe in prayer over medicine, and in fairy tales making ridiculous claims."

A Christian Response

How should Christians respond to scientific positivism? How much truth is there to the position? Despite that scientific evidence is the reigning paradigm in our culture, it fails on many points, the most obvious one of which is this: The statement "Something is only true if it can be proved by science" is not provable by science. That is a philosophical statement, not a scientific one. By definition, the very foundation of the template is self-defeating.

It also fails when we consider that most of the things we know in life are not subject to scientific proof: I like apple pie, I forgive you, I felt chilly yesterday, I saw a beautiful sunset five days ago, when I was in California I saw a double rainbow (A double rainbow!), I have a stomachache, Bill is my friend, that wasn't fair, I'm in love with Denise, I'm afraid of heights, my favorite movie is Gladiator, I feel at peace with myself, that makes me angry, I prefer rock music to opera, I think Jimmy Fallon is funny, I believe there should be some kind responsible gun control. There are thousands, if not tens of thousands or even millions of these things.

We also know about the existence of things that we can't touch, taste, feel, hear or see. They are not empirically testable or verifiable in a lab: time, peace, justice, love, memory, reason, and values, to name a few. There are disciplines that have nothing to do with science, but are still valid knowledge: jurisprudence, economics, history, literature, politics, music appreciation, philosophy, theology, and logic.

Science Doesn't Own Knowledge

As it turns out, probably most of what we know is not subject to scientific experimentation, empirical verification, or can be considered scientific knowledge. It is both illogical and unreasonable to apply scientific reasoning to any of these matters—so also to the existence of God, the veracity of miracles and the reliability of the Biblical text. While we can bring some scientific thinking to bear as we evaluate them, they are just as much outside of the purview of science as "I forgive you."

And yet this movement in our society is causing many people to doubt the metaphysical, conceptual, abstract, and transcendent realities of our lives. Ironically, those who fear gullibility are being sucked into the web of deceit. Dr. Evandro Agazzi, President of the International Academy of Philosophy and Science in Brussels, gave a paper presenting more evidence contrary to the logical positivism paradigm. He said (and this is not an exact quote):

In the realm of science, one person will make flat statements that the world exists, and yet the same person would say they believe God exists. Why should we use different wording? It all goes back to a principle of authority. Our view of science as an authority causes us to talk about material things as existence but non-material things as simply our opinions or beliefs. Yet the moral law within us exists just as surely as the stars in the heavens. Space is filled with places that have a particular purpose (even sometimes empty spaces), and therefore they exist—they are impregnated with meaning that differentiates one place from the other place. There is material homogeneity (a similarity made up of atoms and molecules), but not homogeneity of purpose or role. And what about time? Time also has "places," and in time we have distinct events so much so that each has its own purpose as well. Special events have no homogeneity—each is unique as it exists in a moment in time. In space and time the distinctive places that exist are identified in relative terms. They all exist relative to me, the person, or to you. With regard to time, you cannot speak about the present unless there is someone who is perceiving it and living in it who says "Now". So, in the same way, time is relative to us. Present, past and future do not exist in physics; they exist in our experience only in relation to us. Heaven, earth, and time all have a religious sense and a personal sense—and that is why they really exist. Principles of physics are delimited (defined) for the sake of objectivity.

But principles of physics cannot and do not cover the whole of reality. Metaphysics have always existed alongside of physics, and are needed to fill in the totality of reality. Never in history were these things seen as mutually exclusive. Humans always seek to give sense and value to their life. Belief and knowledge together make up the totality of reality; science cannot have ultimate authority because it is only one slice of reality.

Summary

Despite the wonders of science and the magnificent benefits available to all of us, science does not and cannot commandeer all knowledge. There are so many elements outside of the scope of science that can truly be considered knowledge that we must question the very foundation of science's claims that if something can't be proved scientifically it is not true. Instead, Christians need to subscribe to truth as being based in reasoning, intuitions, faith, the revelation of God, trustworthy testimony, experiences, and scientific facts.

Discussion Questions

1. Think about how so many disciplines are trying to jump on the "science" bandwagon. What are examples of academic disciplines that call themselves "sciences" that aren't truly sciences?
2. Why is the foundation of science as the basis of all knowledge so appealing?
3. Give other examples of things we know that are not able to be evaluated in a science laboratory.

4. Why do some atheists evaluate Christians as being "intellectually dishonest"? What do you think they are perceiving?

5. If you were in a conversation with someone who kept demanding "Prove it to me," what recourse do you have in reply that will persuade them that all knowledge is not scientific?

3

||||||||||||||||||||||||||||||||||||||||||||||||||||||||||||||||||||||||||||||||||||||||||||||

ALGORITHMIC FLUX: THE NEW CONSTANT

The other day I went to book a hotel room. I checked the rates, but they're different on every website. I called the hotel itself, and those rates are different, too. I shut down my search and returned to it a few hours later, and the prices were all different yet again from just a few hours before. It's the same way with plane seats and rental car rates. The industry now uses algorithms to set prices, and those prices change with every conditional alteration. When a seat is bought or a room is rented, or when a minute passes and therefore the timing of sales, the computer makes new calculations and the whole pricing landscape changes. It's a little bit like the "Butterfly Effect," an idea that if a butterfly flaps its wings in Brazil it could set off a chain of events resulting in a tornado in Indonesia. This principle is what makes the weather ultimately not completely predictable, because there are so many variables in the mix that it's impossible to control and forecast all of them.

Our society is becoming so dependent on computer-driven algorithms that algorithmic flux is the new constant. Facebook's news feed, along with Twitter and Instagram, weather forecasting, Snapchat—almost everything that you do with a computer relies in some way on an algorithm. In practical terms, they help us process information in ways that were never before possible, but the other side of the coin is that they are used by industries to create situations that may maximize profits and reduce empty rooms and seats, but at the same time destabilize our knowledge. Inconsistency and instability are the new normal. We cannot assume a plane seat will be the same price from one minute to the next. All has become relative.

Relativism Becomes Objective

This reality of algorithmic flux is illustrative of the second comprehensive paradigm of our age: relativism. In the writings of existentialist philosopher Søren Kierkegaard, this was known as the "teleological suspension of the ethical"—that right and wrong are not absolutes but depend on the purpose behind them. Joseph Fletcher popularized the philosophy in his seminal work in 1966 called Situation Ethics.[14] "The situationist enters into every decision-making situation fully armed with the ethical maxims of his community and its heritage, and he treats them with respect as illuminators of his problems. Just the same he is prepared in any situation to compromise them or set them aside in the situation if love seems better served by doing so."[15] Essentially it's an algorithmic approach to life: truth and morality change and flow according to each situation, with no particular

---

[14] Joseph Fletcher, Situation Ethics: The New Morality (Philadelphia, PA: Westminster Press, 1966)

[15] Ibid. p. 26

objective standard or stabilizing reference point. Whatever the situation calls for becomes the criteria for decision, and what is "right" and "true" could depend upon the particular perspectives or values of each observer or participant. The basis of morality and values becomes societal advancement or individual well-being, as defined by each society or individual.

I have been told, "What Hitler did was only wrong because the Germans lost the war. It was 'morality by force.' Hitler didn't think of himself as evil. If you were a member of the Nazi party in World War II, it is possible that the extermination of the Jews was considered to be morally acceptable. Our assessment of the evil of it is based on our own subjective assessment. Morality is not derived only from personal opinions and beliefs, but also from a society to which a person belongs. All morality is, or should be, simply described as socially acceptable action. If everyone can't agree on what evil is, it proves there is no such thing as objective morality."[16]

Another blogger wrote, "Wellbeing is the only reasonable reference point because there is no way to demonstrate what god thinks about morality or what his rules are. Also the only moral rules that are generally agreed upon outside of any particular religion are all related to human wellbeing. So even though the most accurate meaning of a word would not depend on whether it is too easily a contrivance of opinion, I think that claiming god decides morality is far worse in this regard. Nobody can demonstrate what god thinks or what his rules are, so under this model nobody knows anything about what I find moral or not. It is totally dependent on each individual's beliefs about what they think god wants."[17]

---

[16] Summary of a post on www.the3rdchoice.org

[17] J Lord on reddit.com

Some people criticize relativism, claiming that a relativist is always wandering because he'll never know if he's right. But if you speak with a true relativist, he'll tell you that the real strength of relativism is a total lack of guilt, because he can never be wrong.

We see this relativism playing itself out not only in the rejection of objective moral standards but also in a modern example of legislation about homosexual rights and practice, where love becomes the final criterion for what is right. When questioned whether or not love should be the standard for the legitimization of incest, child sexual abuse, or bigamy, the response I have been given is: "Evoking incest is beside the point. No one is seeking to legislate marriage among family members. But if there is concern about the 'slippery slope' into incest, then that slope begins with the very idea of marriage, so we should scrap the institution altogether (if we are worried about incest)."[18]

Relativism claims that the right and the good cannot possibly depend on an unknown God, high in the sky by and by, who can't be consulted with and who doesn't speak. The only reliable standard is what we can know and can see: ourselves. Like shooting an arrow into a target on an airplane, it matters not that the target is moving because we are moving with it. When society moves, definitions of the good and the right move in tandem, it is claimed, so we can all live together as one happy family (except those who insist on an unmovable objective standard,[19] and their ideas must be suppressed for the well-being of all).

While relativism (nothing is really true) and positivism (science is all that is true) might seem to contradict each other,

---

[18] a post on www.the3rdchoice.org

[19] many Christians believe in an unmovable, objective standard

they are in perfect agreement because of the scope of each. Once I was in conversation with a teenager who insisted there was no such thing as truth. So I said, "Suppose I walked into Sears, and all the merchandise said 'SEARS' on it, and all the employees had 'SEARS' name tags, and they got their paychecks from SEARS, and the big sign on the outside of the store said SEARS, but I believed I was in JC Penneys, was I in Penneys because that's what I believed?" She answered yes. I was astounded. I pressed her, and used a math illustration—suppose I firmly believed that $2+2=5$, would that make it so? She said yes, but her resolve was wavering. I asked if I believed the moon was made of blue cheese (a scientific example), would that make it so? Finally she caved and said, "OK, OK. I have thought about this further now. Truth applies to math and science, but to nothing else, especially religion." The belief is that objective truth is in the realm of science and math only; everything else is relative. The problem lies in the contradiction: Is there such a thing as objective truth or isn't there? Their answer: it depends. Relativity tells them what is objective and what is not, which is a complete contradiction. In other words, they choose to live with the paradox, accepting both contradictory positions as "true."

A Christian Response

How should Christians respond to relativism? How much truth is there to the position? Despite that individual preference is the reigning paradigm in our culture, it fails on many points, the most obvious one of which is this: "If you say there is no such thing as objective truth, can you assure me that perspective is objectively true?" By definition, the very foundation of the template is self-defeating.

Relativism also fails because it becomes not only impossible but contrary to the relativistic ideal to campaign for moral reform. Heroes of our culture, like Dr. Martin Luther King Jr. and Mahatma Gandhi, have no place on the pedestal of honor because they were resisting the flow of society's (the majority's) definition of wellbeing. Moral reform is a misguided effort if all goodness and right is defined by majority rule.

In addition, relativism fails because then all definitions of harmful oppression are mere opinions, and if another individual or society perceives them differently, then are they really harmful or evil? Who is to say that Hitler was wrong, because wrong is in the definition of the definer. Rape, child sexual abuse, and human trafficking are then merely perceptions of wrong by people who think such. Given the ubiquity of pornography and human trafficking in our era, relativist would have to concede that the opinion of the majority would allow them to continue. There is money to be made and pleasure to be had, so who gets to decide what qualifies as "the wellbeing of society"?

A final failure of relativism is that if all points of view are equally valid, then truth is self-contradictory because many points of view contradict other points of view. Truth, right, and wrong, and even wellbeing all become meaningless terms, and therefore justice becomes a meaningless term and concept, and society cannot function without the foundations of truth, right, wrong, justice, trust and honesty.

Summary

While relativism allows us to make decisions contingent on individual situations, it is an inadequate ground for ultimate truth. Wellbeing is a noble pursuit and a high value, but God's character is the only fundamental basis for objective truth.

Discussion Questions

1. Can you explain how relativism is self-refuting?
2. What are the benefits of relativism? Why do you think our society has leaned in this direction?
3. How have Christians themselves been pulled into the relativistic camp and even share some of this mindset?
4. Is there any relativism that is legitimate? (Is it ever right to say, "It depends"?)
5. How do we distinguish, then, between "wrong" relativism and "right" relativism?

4

||||||||||||||||||||||||||||||||||||||||||||||||||||||||||||||||||||||||||||||||||||||||||||

SEXUAL EXPRESSION: THE NEW "UNIMORALITY"

Sexual morality has taken on many new faces just in the past few years. We know that the sexual revolution of the 1960s concentrated on college campuses. Watchwords of the day were "Anything Goes" and "Drugs, Sex, and Rock and Roll". Feminism, gay rights campaigners, and free love were all part of the social picture. Studies have shown that between 1965 and 1974 the number of women engaging in premarital sex showed a marked increase,[20] along with the proliferation of a world of new sexually transmitted diseases. It was only the beginning of a new sexual climate.

In 1973 Roe v Wade legalized abortion, since there was a growing demand for abortion based on how many women were

---

[20] "The Impact of the Female Marriage Squeeze and the Contraceptive Revolution on Sex Roles and the Women's Liberation Movement in the United States, 1960 to 1975", David M. Heer; Amyra Grossbard-Shechtman, Journal of Marriage and the Family, Vol. 43, No. 1. (February 1981), pp. 49–65

conceiving unwanted children, mostly outside of marriage. Sexual expression was becoming more common in magazines, but primarily on the television and in movies. Boundaries were being pushed, and the effort to restrain them was only half-hearted. Children were being raised under the umbrella of a much looser sexual morality than that of previous generations, and so a new normal was being created.

LGBT social movements (which had begun in the early 20th century[21]) became more visible, particularly in the 1970s and 80s. Anyone who disagreed with the movement was slandered as psychologically deranged with the label of "homophobic." In 1983 homosexuality was decriminalized.

We all know how things have progressed to get us where we are today. Morals were loosened, religion declined, and the Bible was not as much recognized as authoritative. Same sex marriage was framed as an issue of rights, not of morality. Couples living together before marriage became commonplace, and efforts to keep sex sacred were ridiculed as Puritanical and repressive. In 2015 same sex marriage became legal in the United States.

Morality Is Redefined

We have gotten to the place where there is a single unofficial sexual morality, what I've chosen to call "unimorality," and that is "I get to do what I want." Hardly any rules or values still stand. The argument for sexual liberty is framed in terms of love and rights, not of morality and right, and the younger generations are buying into it. After all, who could be against love and rights? Anyone who expresses disagreement is shamed, slandered, and sometimes even shouted down. It's rule, not of law, but of intimidation. Actors who speak out against the unimorality

---

[21] In 1924, the first gay rights organization in America was founded by Henry Gerber

are summarily fired, as are teachers and even businessmen. Companies refusing to tow the line are boycotted.

It's a new fundamentalism that has been percolating in the U.S. for several decades, but only recently has garnered enough cultural victories to push harder for their ideologies. It is grounded in tolerance, morality and knowledge, but all three of those terms have been redefined to suit the unimoral agenda. Tolerance is now "acceptance of those who agree with our position;" morality is now "the value system of the masses;" and knowledge is "anything that science can prove." These definitions thrive because, as any authoritarian government of the previous century proves, definitions belong to the power bloc. But they also thrive because people can sometimes be mindless followers. When the media, academia, politicians, and the judiciary all conform to doublespeak as the standard of correctness, the culture of objective truth, objective morality, and genuine freedom is commandeered and waylaid.

The victim of this cultural tyranny in our era is Christianity, much as the victims of social evolution in the 1930s and 40s were the Jews. Christianity is actively being marginalized into a pathology (...phobia), a mythology, an immorality (the only sin of our era is unacceptance of the new fundamentalism), and intolerance (refusing to conform to the agenda of the new fundamentalism). Under the guise of cultural progress...

1. Only voices that conform to the fundamentalist agenda are allowed to be heard. We are becoming a Stepford society.

2. Exercise of conscience and conscientious objection has become criminalized.

3. Any objections or disapproval of the new sexual morality are labeled with the redefined terms of "racism," "intolerance," and "phobia".

The goal of the new fundamentalism is nothing less than total cultural domination by way of tyranny, redefinition, and suppression. But tolerance that doesn't go both ways is just a guise for repression, and redefinition is a classic authoritarian strategy of power and control.

What is at stake is the very foundation of a tolerant and pluralistic free society, and what is in the crosshairs is Christianity. Now is the time for Christians to rise up to cultural engagement. As Dr. Martin Luther King, Jr. said, "The ultimate tragedy is not the oppression and cruelty by the bad people but the silence over that by the good people."

Tolerance is Redefined

Ironically, the only value in the unimorality is tolerance, yet the movement is intolerant of disagreement and opposition. We need to understand, however, that tolerance can never be complete. There are always two sides. To tolerate one thing is to not tolerate another. If I tolerate free speech, I may also be tolerating hate speech or bigotry. If I tolerate a religion that kills animals, I may also be tolerating animal abuse. It's impossible to tolerate all things and all people, because a decision in one direction is also a decision in other directions. Any choice to tolerate one thing may also be a decision not to tolerate its polar opposite. Thus, tolerance is always selective, and therefore both biased and political.

No matter what, it still comes down to priorities and values. While I respect the ideal of being tolerant and respectful of positions, behaviors, and values different than my own, I also have to understand that tolerance of everything is not only impossible but also foolish. Ultimately, we all have to live by values deeper than political correction, respectful tolerance, and individual rights. We have to live by overarching standards that give meaning and boundaries to respectful behavior, tolerance, and rights.

The Christian Response

How should Christians respond to unimorality? How much truth is there to the position? Despite that tolerance is the reigning paradigm in our culture, it fails on many points, the most obvious one of which is this: "How can a movement founded on tolerance be intolerant of conscientious objection?" By definition, the very foundation of the template is self-defeating.

Christians should respond to unimorality with love for people, a firm stance against sin, a grounding in the truth, and an overarching tolerance. First let's talk generally about love for people. Jesus gave us no other option. No one can point to a Scripture, or an example in Jesus, where we learn "It's OK not to love this person." We are to love even our enemies, even those who persecute us, even those who despitefully use us. When we are to discipline sinners in the church (such as in 1 Corinthians 5), even the actions Paul demands that we take are ultimately actions of love. Even while we were sinners, Christ died for us, for God so loved the world…

Secondly, as Christians we realize that we must take a firm stance against sin. The call to love never once in the Bible changed the definition of sin. The Bible doesn't give just one definition of sin, but it's a multi-faceted concept. "Sin is thinking, doing, or being anything that demonstrates a dissatisfaction with God." "Sin is declaring ourselves the arbiters of right and wrong, rather than living in a dependent relationship." "Sin is humanity's enmity against God consisting in his refusal to understand and will what is right." "Sin refers to our human propensity to mess things up." In the Bible sin has been variously defined and is not just a simple picture. Sin is a state of being, an orientation, and a behavior. Sin is missing the mark, making mistakes, rebellion, perversion, evil, and trouble. Sin is any lack of conformity to the moral law of God. And love never changes any of that. It changes how we treat people, but never what sin is and how it is defined.

Third, as Christians we must always be firmly grounded in the truth. The Bible insists on it, and we subscribe to truth as it is revealed in the Bible. While the advocates of unimorality may intimidate with word campaigns and signs designed to make disagreement sound like lunacy ("Love Wins"), our morality is grounded in the nature and character of God, not in noble-sounding clichés. Objective morality is humanity living by the unchangeable standard of God's transcendent nature, not by paradigm of algorithmic flux. True morality is not the expression of principled self-interest, but a universal code built into all of the universe by our immutable God.

Lastly, we must still be a people of tolerance, because we live in a pluralistic society founded on the rights and freedoms of a very diverse population of people. At the bottom line, Christians are most likely some of the most tolerant people on the planet. I think we can all agree that a person has no need to be tolerant of something unless they object to it. If I already accept it, or don't care about, I don't need to tolerate it, because it requires nothing of me. People who agree with homosexual orientation, expression, and relationships in all its forms don't have to tolerate it, since they have no objection to it. Tolerance only comes into the picture when I come across a person or an issue that I have disagreements with. This picture is a growing reality for Christians in America.

The Most Tolerant: Those With the Strongest Beliefs

If tolerance, then, by definition, requires an initial objection, then conservatives, ironically enough, may be much more tolerant than liberals, since there are so many more things to which they object. And Christians find themselves in a culture and society where tolerance has to be continually practiced, since the Bible tells us we are in the world, not of it, and the wheat and weeds will grow together, and the sheep and goats co-exist, and it is not our place to judge those outside of the Church (1 Cor. 5.12). Think about Jesus, and the people and groups and actions he never spoke out against, and we see how tolerance works in a Christian worldview.

So if tolerance requires that I object to something, it also implies that I don't always do something about it. I withhold power. If I would stop something if I could, but am powerless to do so, I am not tolerant, merely impotent. True tolerance means I could exercise power to stop it, but voluntarily withhold that power. Christians do this all the time. We don't shoot people who disagree with us; we don't run them out of office; we don't burn their stores. We are taught to turn the other cheek, take the hit, and walk the extra mile. We hold back, as we rightly should. Otherwise we would be like ISIS, burning, looting, and killing everything in our path that disagrees with our theology or "sacred" lifestyle.

Relativism, as discussed in chapter three, takes the position that anything goes: We have a multitude of views, values, and practices all around us, and therefore we draw the conclusion that there is no justifiable way to choose among them, because truth is merely opinion. Tolerance, by contrast, characterizes us as Christians. Sure, we object to those views, and we do have the power to (possibly) stop it, but we withhold that power out of respect for the right of the other person to hold that position. We learn to live side by side in love with those with whom we disagree.

As I said before, no moral person tolerates everything. It comes down to values. There are tragic issues around us—racism, human trafficking, rape, child sexual abuse, economic injustice, the exploitation of women—where freedom of expression and justice collide. Given that everyone (I hope) agrees that some things should not be tolerated, the real issue should not be whether one is tolerant or intolerant, but what's included on one's list.

Thus conservative Christians may possibly be the most tolerant people in our country, and that's a value for us to recognize because of the high and powerful objections Christians have to the direction and expressions of the culture. And yet Christians, by the Holy Spirit, show considerable respect and even love for those who hold those positions, despite our disagreement. Our commission is to love one another and make disciples, not to judge—to stand against sin, to be grounded in the truth, and also to be some of the most tolerant people of our country.

Christians, then, are not guilty of intolerance, due to the nature of our own ideology. We subscribe to truth as it is revealed in the Bible, and while we think that those who believe otherwise are holding on to falsehood, we still live next to each other in harmony all across the nation. Christians do have the public and social force to protest more than we do, and yet we most often withhold that action.

We reject the unimorality, and we continue to work both publicly and personally for the true morality, for objective standards conforming to objective truth, and for justice in our country built on biblical principles. At the same time we are people of love and tolerance, winning the world to Christ with a message of reconciliation, not one of hate.

Summary

Tolerance is being redefined to manipulate society into a secular humanist culture. Christians need to be aware of the power of words and to construct a vocabulary of morality and truth.

Discussion Questions:

1. Why is well-being an inadequate foundation for deciding morality?
2. How can we advocate for morality without coming across as judgmental?
3. How do Christians show our tolerance in this pluralistic society?
4. Christians need to think of words to counteract the placards on the street. What are truthful and loving words we can use to reply to campaigns that read "No Hate," "Love Wins," and "Equality for All"?

5

||||||||||||||||||||||||||||||||||||||||||||||||||||||||||||||||||||||||||||||||||||||||

TECHNOLOGY:
THE NEW UNIVERSAL

Hardly anything needs to be said to convince anyone that our era will go down in history as the technological revolution, following the industrial revolution of the 19th century and the printing revolution (The Gutenberg Revolution) of the 1450s. Our society—no, the whole world—is transformed almost daily by new advances brought to us by the marvelous capabilities of computer technology. This revolution was forecast by Alvin Toffler in Future Shock (1970). He spoke of the accelerative thrust of technology, so much so that the rate of change would increase to the point that our imaginations wouldn't be able to keep up.[22] The technological engine that would drive change was seen to be the computer, even before personal computers were invented.[23] Toffler predicted that knowledge would fuel

---

[22] An idea proposed by C.P. Snow, novelist and scientist, quoted in Alvin Toffler, Future Shock (Toronto, Canada: Bantam Books, 1970), p. 22

[23] Toffler, Op. Cit. p. 29

the revolution. Little did he know what the next forty years would bring.

John Naisbitt, in Megatrends (1982), observed that we were moving rapidly from an industrial society to an information society.[24] Naisbitt affirmed Toffler's insights that knowledge would be the new wealth and the source of power. And here we are in the 21st century, watching these predictions and observations come true all around us, accelerating the pace of change and the growth of information daily. Technology rules the world. Between our computers, tablets, and smart phones, we might as well insert a metaphorical technological IV needle into our veins and live by technology. Not only is information power, but information and connectedness have become life.

Who Needs Whom?

It's easy to see that the paradigm of technology is changing the way we think, work, communicate, recreate, vacation, and study. Computers are not just changing the speed of our lives, but also its very nature. It has invaded every corner of our lives, from banking to buying, and research to relaxation. Jacques Ellul said, "No social, human, or spiritual fact is so important as the fact of [technology] in the modern world. And yet no subject is so little understood." In the second movie of the Matrix trilogy (The Matrix Reloaded, 2003), Neo is engaged with Councilor Harmann in a conversation about the place of technology in our lives:

> **Councilor Harmann:** Down here, sometimes
> I think about all those people still plugged into

---

[24] John Naisbitt, Megatrends: Ten New Directions Transforming Our Lives (New York, NY: Warner Books, 1982), chapter 1, pp. 1-33

the Matrix and when I look at these machines I... I can't help thinking that in a way... we are plugged into them.

Neo: But we control these machines; they don't control us.

Councilor Harmann: Of course not. How could they? The idea is pure nonsense. But... it does make one wonder... just... what is control?

Neo: If we wanted, we could shut these machines down.

Councilor Harmann: [Of] course. That's it. You hit it. That's control, isn't it? If we wanted we could smash them to bits. Although, if we did, we'd have to consider what would happen to our lights, our heat, our air...

Neo: So we need machines and they need us, is that your point, Councilor?

Councilor Harmann: No. No point. Old men like me don't bother with making points. There's no point.

Neo: Is that why there are no young men on the council?

Councilor Harmann: Good point.

We have brought technology to the point where it seems our very lives depend on it—technology has become life. Who controls whom? Is technology our servant, or are we its? Originally we dreamed that technology would make life easier, but actually the technology has added to so much clutter in our lives that the noise of life has gotten oppressive, and while things are so much better, they are also at the same time so much worse. We have so many things coming at us continually, with so many directions to turn, and so much of which we must keep informed that we succumb to overload.

Research shows that technological overload, giving us too many choices and too much information, quickly brings us to a place where we hit a wall, and the oversaturation becomes counter-productive. Faced with 120 choices of the product we are searching for on the Internet, we tend to stop processing information effectively, cease being discerning, and use our intuitions and emotions to make a choice, even though we know it may not be the most logical decision. Logic fails from mental exhaustion, and overstimulation creates under-thinking.

Taking all this together, technology is really a paradigm of knowledge in our world. Almost all of our knowledge comes from technological sources (namely, the world wide web), and because the amount of information is overwhelming, we generally skim a few articles, surf for more, make a decision, and move on. Such is the state of knowledge in far too many cases; we are guilty of being proverbial "sophomores" (wise fools). We have come to the point where we know so much, we know close to nothing. We live one inch deep in most parts of our lives, because that's all we have time to process.

John Naisbitt said, "We are drowning in information but starved for knowledge."[25] The amount of information is so

---

[25] Naisbitt, Op. Cit. p. 17

immense it is no longer a resource, but a chaotic detriment—"information pollution".[26] Google was originally designed to help us find and process information, but the quantity of websites and the sheer bulk of information often necessitates that we only bother with the first couple pages of a Google search, and move on.

A Christian Response

How should Christians respond to this paradigm of knowledge? How much truth is there to the position? Despite that technology is the reigning paradigm in our culture, it fails on many points, the most obvious one of which is this: The overwhelming abundance of information has caused a drastic reduction in knowledge. By definition, the very foundation of the template is self-defeating.

While it may sound primitive in our wild and wonderful world of technological resources, Christians need to slow our pace, take at least occasional and deliberate respite from technology, find a place for spiritual discipline, and take time to breathe nature and life.

Mary Pipher, in The Shelter of Each Other: Rebuilding Our Families,[27] says that technology, despite its wonderful benefits, has overstimulated us to the point of exhaustion and disconnection, and what we need most sometimes is protected time, space, and personal (not digital) connection.[28] As a clinical psychologist, Dr. Pipher has observed that taking teenagers away from technology and putting them in nature for times of respite

---

[26] Ibid. p. 17

[27] Ballantine Books, 1996

[28] Mary Pipher, The Shelter of Each Other: Rebuilding Our Families (New York, NY: Ballantine Books, 1996) p. 56

does wonders to make them less anxious, more communicative, more emotionally stable, and more relational. Pipher says, "The speed of change is as dizzying as our lack of reflection on its consequences. ... TV isolates people in their leisure time. ... Many children have been conditioned via the media into having highly dysfunctional attention spans."[29] Such is the nature of knowledge under the technological paradigm.

Billy Graham, in a 1998 crusade, said, "The information age may go down in history as the period when our culture forgot the most important thing: That our souls need to breathe and grow. We're separated from God."

It's an old concept, but we need recreation to be re-created. As the hymn says, "Take time to be holy." It has been proved over and over that a walk in the woods, taking time to pray, attending worship (and shutting out the cares of life for one hour), spending time actually digesting the Word of God, reading good books, and meditating on the things of God can lead us to lives of genuine knowledge, shunning the shallowness of our culture and feasting on the true riches of deep thought.

Summary

Technology is a fantastic boon to culture, and has many promises of benefits for the whole planet. Christians need to temper their acceptance of technology, however, based on the values taught in Scripture and the straight edge of godly, objective morality. Every movement has its pros and cons, and technology is no different. We must all be careful to separate the good from the unhelpful, and not just swallow all technology uncritically.

---

[29] Ibid. pp. 89-91

Discussion Questions

1. How do we decide between "moral" and "immoral" technology?
2. Since the progress and drive of technology is poised only to increase and not decrease, what standards do we use to make future decisions about what technology to adopt and what to reject, while avoiding the "Amish Syndrome," where we would stop the clock at a particular time and refuse any further progression regardless of its value?
3. What strategies can you take to be able to take reasonable Sabbaths from technology? What do you consider to be the advantages of such practice?

6

||||||||||||||||||||||||||||||||||||||||||||||||||||||||||||||||||||||||||||||||||||||||

SOCIAL MEDIA: THE NEW SELF-IMAGE

After the turbulent 60s, the 1970s kids became known as the "Me Generation." They were followed in 80s by the Me-Me Generation, and in the 90s by the Me-ME-and-only MEEEEEE kids. Several generations now have been raised with an unrealistic sense of entitlement, an artificially exaggerated self-esteem, and a climate so rewarding and affirming that it has stripped children of any realistic sense of self. Add to that the wonders of technology and the advent of social media, and we are seeing a new paradigm of narcissism that even young Narcissus wouldn't recognize. He fell in love with his own image in a pool of water, but can you imagine his self-preoccupation if he had a cell phone and a selfie stick? We need not imagine, for we just need to observe a group of teenagers at an event.

Nancy Jo Sales, in her book <u>American Girls: Social Media and the Secret Lives of Teenagers</u>,[30] shows us that social media such as Facebook (Snapchat, Instagram) is far beyond a mere way for kids to connect with each other. Social media and selfies are the shape of modern self-image—self-branding, a technological means to garner recognition of oneself.

The problem, of course, is that it places self-image totally into the realm of image, thoroughly removed from any notion of character. Back in the ancient days, like before 1970, character was the value to be sought after as we shaped our personalities and priorities. With the progress of television and a breakdown of any corporate morality, advertising was targeted at children and teens, specifically to convince them that they were inadequate without products, that changing their looks was their greatest need, and that their appearance trumped their inner self. This strategy was reinforced by the expansion of the celebrity culture, where what mattered was getting one's face in a public place. Now we have "progressed" to the point where we can text and share pictures with each other via smartphone instantly and continually, in an effort to create a personal "brand"—a self-image consisting wholly of image, regardless of substance. The inexplicable Kardashian phenomenon is the perfect example. What do they do except pose for pictures?

Jean Twenge, in <u>Generation Me</u>, states that today's young Americans are more confident, assertive and entitled than any previous generation—and more miserable than ever before.[31] She argues that the trend toward self has resulted in the decline of social rules (someone else telling one how to behave), of organized religion (an authority above one), and of academic performance (an effort to develop an inner quality). The most

---

[30] A Borzoi book published by Alfred A. Knopf, 2016

[31] Jean M. Twenge, <u>Generation Me</u> (New York, NY: Free Press, 2006)

obvious results have been anxiety, depression, laziness, stress, and sexual experimentation.

Real Artificiality

This situation has created a paradigm characterized by artificiality. We are a plastic culture, fiercely independent and self-oriented. It plays itself out in our shallow knowledge, relativistic perspective, and egocentric alignment of personal morality. In a sense, the 60s have come back again in a new and even less weighty form. Back then it was "Don't trust anyone over 30." Now it's "Don't trust anyone. I am all that matters." There is a significant disregard for any authority, any wisdom, and any experience. There is no authority except one's own, and even that is an artificial authority: all show with no core, like a cheap, hollow, plastic toy.

A Christian Response

How should Christians respond to the artificiality of the social media self? How much truth is there to the position? Despite that celebrity-image is the reigning paradigm in our culture, it fails on many points, the most obvious one of which is this: "How can a self-image devoid of substance be substantial enough to achieve the tasks of a healthy personality?" By definition, the very foundation of the template is self-defeating.

By contrast, our Christian worldview says that we are significant and profound, created in the image of God to grow in character and knowledge to be conformed to the likeness of Jesus. The only course we can chart, besides blind conformity to the destructive trends, is to adapt a totally counter-cultural mindset and strategy. It used to be that parents spent their time teaching their children how to be productive members of society by training them in the ways of the prevailing culture; now our wisest choice is to teach our children how to be productive and healthy by protecting them from the culture. It's at least one of the reasons the homeschool movement has accelerated: we fear for the next generation, especially our own children. While the City of Man has never been the City of God, the artificiality of the current reigning paradigm threatens to strip the next generation of some of the few elements that make society work: character and integrity.

Instead, we need a self-image founded in the character of God and our significance in His image. Who we are inside is more important than who we are outside. We establish our value by godly character, not by the quantity and quality of our selfie shots. Of course, we all know this. The next generation doesn't.

"There are no ordinary people. You have never talked to a mere mortal. Nations, cultures, arts, civilizations—these are mortal, and their life is to ours as the life of a gnat. But it is with immortals whom we joke with, work with, marry, snub, and exploit—immortal horrors or everlasting splendors."[32] The Christian response is to be and raise "everlasting splendors".

Summary

We must beware not to fall for the lies of culture as if they are merely cute and innocent. We are not of this world. Christians must continue to train our children and students (and remind ourselves as adults) that character trumps image and integrity supersedes impressions.

---

[32] C.S. Lewis, The Weight of Glory

Discussion Questions

1. While we know that impressions are important, and the way we come across counts, how can we strike a balance between emphasizing impressions and developing character?
2. What are strategies we can use to develop character in our children despite the pounding influence of our culture that image is what is important?
3. Is it helpful to develop a list stating at what ages certain technologies are healthy for children, or is such a list either useless or counter-productive?

7

||||||||||||||||||||||||||||||||||||||||||||||||||||||||||||||||||||||||||||||||||||||||||

POINTS:
THE NEW CURRENCY

An odd phenomenon has secretly become a new paradigm in America. More than a decade ago, credit card companies began offering reward points for purchases made that could be used for merchandise or cash back. Then the retailers, hotels, and airlines started to get in on the act, realizing that people were willing to spend real money to acquire the alternate currency of "points". Not long ago my wife and I were sitting through a sales pitch for a time-share property, except that the industry is shying away from the time-share concept and is now selling "points". One is expected to pay a lump sum, not for a real estate footprint any more, but to register to be able to buy points. And then there are various plans where one can buy an agreed-upon quantity of points that can be used for a variety of goods and services. When I mentioned to the salesperson that formerly with time-shares, one was at least buying a week of real estate, for which one would receive a deed, I was told that the whole time-share/ deed/footprint concept was passé, and that for my $30,000 I would be registered to purchase points to use for travel and vacations anywhere in the world. I said to my wife, "They want us to buy air for the privilege of buying more air." "Oh, no," we were assured, "your points can be used to buy real goods and services."

"And what if I want to sell my plan 20 years from now because I'm done with it? An owner used to be able to sell their time-share deed to a new owner, and at least recoup some money from it. What if the plan isn't working for me and I want out?"

"Um, you can try to sell it, but there's nothing to sell. A new owner would have to buy their own points."

Bingo. "You want me to buy air."

Realistically speaking, then, points are not a false currency, because any element that can be traded for goods counts as currency. It's just that points are non-existent and meaningless, and are only defined by their context.

A Meaningless Reference Point

Philosophically speaking, this is called a reference point. A reference point is a stable standard allowing a person to reason and progress with purpose: the North Star, a mountain in the distance, a common location in geometry, a baseline measurement in science or medicine, or even a starting line in a race or project. We need something reliable by which to measure. In philosophy, it is often said that the particulars (the small things, the details) are defined by the universals—I only know what a leaf is because I know what a tree is; a leg only has meaning as part of a body. Others might claim that the universals are defined by the particulars: What's a tree without leaves?

Regardless, there is always a context and a reference point if there is going to be meaning.

"Points" are a paradigm without a reference point, like life without a reference point. We buy and sell, laugh and cry, but where's the meaning of it all? It's like being alone in a small boat, without oars or rudder, in the middle of the ocean in a deep fog. Without a reference point, you are lost. We need stars, or a compass, or the sun, or something to give us our bearings. I think it's safe to say we've all been in a situation where we were lost, and we have to stop and get our bearings. We have to find something by which to gauge where we are and where we are trying to go. Without it, all movement, progress, and assessment of value are without purpose. It's a common occurrence that when people are lost in the woods, they unconsciously walk in circles. Without a reference point for guidance, their direction is actually meaningless. Jean-Paul Sartre counseled us that "No finite point has any meaning unless it has an infinite reference point." Wittgenstein[33] argues that the sense of the world must lie outside the world, that man never has sufficient perspective from within this world to build an eternal structure of truth and value. If there is any value that does have value, it must lie outside of the whole sphere of what happens now.

If currencies are arbitrary, subject to algorithmic flux, changeable by power blocks or popular recognition, I can never count on anything, and all transactions become ultimately meaningless except for the arbitrary value I assign for my own context and satisfaction. And while I may save points today, what if tomorrow the currency of vogue is bitcoin or yuan, or even M&Ms? How can I function in a world that is only anchored to "air"?

---

[33] In the Tractatus Logico-Philosophicus

In other words, unlinking our experiences, direction, and value system from anything objective has far-reaching implications for most of life. Atheists with whom I have spoken support this with statements like, "There is nothing in life that has meaning, not even this conversation," and "It doesn't matter what we do, because ultimately nothing matters." When I question them, then, that if they were serious in this assessment, nothing has purpose, there are no rights and no wrongs, no good and bad, and therefore not even any knowledge, they balk. "We needed to manufacture such things to survive." It's all, then, a false front and a charade, a bad joke with no punch line, and the saddest declaration about life that could be imagined.

A Christians Response

How should Christians respond to the floating currency of our time, creating meaning and value in the meaningless and valueless? How much truth is there to the position? Despite that people seem to like the freedom (or the deception) of not dealing in genuine currency, it fails on many points (pun intended), the most obvious one of which is this: "If we are imputing value to the valueless, are we not admitting that we are living a sham?" By definition, the very foundation of the template is self-defeating.

God is our only sufficient reference point. Francis Schaeffer said, "Finite man in the external universe, being finite, has no sufficient reference point if he begins absolutely and autonomously from himself and thus needs certain knowledge. God gives us this in the Scriptures."[34] As Christians, we are acutely aware of our finiteness, limitations, and vulnerabilities, and as such that we are an insufficient reference point for meaning

---

[34] Francis Schaeffer, the God who is there (Downers Grove, IL: Inter-Varsity Press, 1968) p. 93

and value. What gives us meaning is an objective authority, an infinite reference point—an anchor to which life and value can be fastened and by which they can be defined. In other words, if there is such a thing as right and wrong, there must be a standard by which they can be defined and understood. And if there is such a standard, there must be a source of that standard.

There are two directions in which we can go: either we create meaning in the fog (pretend the air means something), or we find some way to get our bearings and make progress. Without an infinite reference point, anyone can make anything whatever he wants, and claim it to be meaningful. But that's a deceptive and self-defeating contradiction. True meaning is found in objective realities, meaning they are outside of ourselves, and are found only in the transcendent, eternal God and his revelation to us in his Word.

Summary

The switch from a somewhat stable and objective currency (dollars) to the totally illusionary "points" is reflective of our culture's move from a rock-solid Christian foundation to the foggy "Neverland" of grounding my decisions and values wherever I want to ground them. Christians look to the character of God and His revelation in the Bible as the foundational rock on which life is built.

Discussion Questions

1. Do you understand the principle of "the particulars are defined by the universals"?
2. Share other examples in life where a reference point is not only useful but necessary.
3. What are proper reference points for believers besides God and the Bible?

8

|||||||||||||||||||||||||||||||||||||||||||||||||||||||||||||||||||||||||||||||||||||||||||

EQUALITY EQUALS QUALITY: THE NEW CURRICULUM

It's not that our educational system is getting lazy, because that's just untrue. Educators are trying very hard to make education work in our culture, to educate the next generation, and to be able to compete on a global scale with the students coming out of the schools of other countries. They keep devising new methods and new strategies, knowing that we have to innovate because the culture and the needs are changing.

It's also true, however, that SAT scores are at their lowest level in 10 years,[35] while some claim that critical reading and math scores have been dropping steadily for the past 50 years.

---

[35] https://www.washingtonpost.com/local/education/sat-scores-at-lowest-level-in-10-years-fueling-worries-about-high-schools/2015/09/02/6b73ec66-5190-11e5-9812-92d5948a40f8_story.html

We read about grade inflation,[36] ironically awarding better grades for worse performances. Combined with the effort to make sure every student feels like a winner, and the resistance to show deference to honor students, American students are getting dumber, if it's not un-politically correct to say so. Some schools are doing away with class rank and the recognition of valedictorians, so students can focus on their accomplishments without comparing themselves to others.[37] The CATO Institute says, "The performance of 17-year-olds has been essentially stagnant across all subjects despite a near tripling of the inflation-adjusted cost of putting a child through the K-12 system. ... America's educational productivity appears to have collapsed."[38]

"Equality Equals Quality"

So why do I call this a paradigm rather than a trend? It's not because making our students more stupid is any kind of goal, but because the educational and socialization model we have deliberately chosen desires to level the playing field in consideration of the more difficult to educate and those who find learning most mystifying—in other words, we are gearing our system to the lowest common denominator in an effort to be all-inclusive, inoffensive and equally rewarding. The result has been a steady decline in intelligence. The paradigm implies that equality equals quality.

The result is students are being educated to pass tests so the teacher and the school do well in comparative analyses and meet quotas. Consequently, a growing percentage of the population

---

[36] http://www.gradeinflation.com

[37] Washington Post, July 13, 2015

[38] http://object.cato.org/sites/cato.org/files/pubs/pdf/pa746.pdf

is working off of inadequate information, which is ironic given that we live in an age of information.

The problem with the paradigm is that the best education is not about equalizing, unifying, and leveling all things so that distinctions and hierarchies are destroyed to bring about a true equality. This is an illusion of progress and a distortion of the ideal education. Instead, true education is a recognition of each person's capabilities, qualities, potential contributions and saturation points, motivating each to do their best while recognizing individual limitations. I'm not trying to write a philosophy of education, but to truly succeed we have to educate to diversity. This does not undermine the equal value of people made in the image of God; it admits that God has gifted us differently.

A Christian Response

How should Christians respond to this notion that the highest quality is to make everyone equal? Despite the recognition that everyone should be treated with dignity and respect, and that everyone should get a chance to be educated to the highest of their capabilities, the paradigm fails on many points, the most obvious one of which is this: Educating to make everyone feel equally recognized and honored fails to recognize and honor the capabilities of the achieving sector, thereby creating a system defined by mediocrity. By definition, the very foundation of the template is self-defeating.

Tony Campolo says, "Nowadays people get an education to get a job to make money to buy stuff they don't need. The purpose of an education is not to get a job. Instead we should get an education to serve people and equip them to serve people in the name of Christ and to share his passionate love. God has created you for something more important than to acquire a lot of things. God created us to do something splendid."[39]

Christians need to educate themselves so that we understand and can explain our worldview, intellectually engage our increasingly God-hostile culture, and be able to "demolish arguments and every pretension that sets itself up against the knowledge of God" (2 Cor. 10.5). J. Gresham Machen said, "False ideas are the greatest obstacles to the reception of the gospel. We may preach with all the fervor of a reformer and yet succeed only in winning a straggler here and there, if we permit the whole collective thought of the nation or of the world to be controlled by ideas which, by the resistless force of logic, prevent Christianity from being regarded as anything more than a harmless delusion. Under such circumstances, what God desires us to do is to destroy the obstacle at its root."

We cannot be a generation of Christians idling in intellectual neutral, letting our minds go to waste,[40] with the arguments of Christianity's detractors going unchallenged. "Intellectual impoverishment with respect to one's faith can thus lead to spiritual impoverishment as well. ... If Christian laymen don't become intellectually engaged, then we are in serious danger of losing our children."[41] According to the Youth Transition Network, 70% of churched youth walk away from the church during their college years. Our culture is flooded with deceptive messages about who God is, who we are, and what is to be valued. People are deluged with lies about life. And we Christians are not doing a good job at substantiating what we believe. An atheist said to me, "Churches offer superficial answers to life's difficult questions." Another told me, "Christianity is bleeding

---

[39] In the video series, "Carpe Diem"

[40] William Lane Craig, Reasonable Faith: Christian Truth and Apologetics (Wheaton, IL: Crossway Books, 1984), p. xiv

[41] Ibid. pp. xiv-xv

because very few young people want to be associated with an institution that is firmly associated with, and in a lot of cases teaches, bigotry and hate."

This intellectual inadequacy needs to rise to a high priority if the church is going to start gaining ground in our increasingly secular culture. We need to be not only grounded in the Word of God, but conversant in the daily news, and able to take stands on moral positions with a vocabulary of truth and power. We need to speak with clarity, conviction, and persistence, show love without anger, authority without browbeating, and superior reasoning instead of comfortable clichés. The Church needs to create a new intellectually-fueled voice, a culturally transforming vocabulary of reconciliation and redemption.

Summary

The point of education is not to be smart so we can get gainful employment and make lots of money. Nor is it to show that we are all alike. The point of education is to equip ourselves to serve God in the world.

Discussion Questions

1. How is it possible to educate unequally according to aptitude while also not isolating or demeaning those students of lesser proficiency?
2. How do these observations pertain to the way we go about Christian Education in the church?
3. Brainstorm ways to use our educations, both ours and our children's, for the kingdom of God and the accomplishment of His will.

9

||||||||||||||||||||||||||||||||||||||||||||||||||||||||||||||||||||||||||||||||||||||

ANGER:
THE NEW ETIQUETTE

It doesn't take a rocket scientist to perceive the escalation of anger in America. Incidents of road rage are only the snow dusting on the mountain peaks of displeasure. School shootings, tragically, are becoming commonplace, along with marathon bombings, theater shootings, church massacres, and even senseless slaughter at a Christmas party, a concert, or a night club. Too many communities share a common bond of grief over pointless killing.

A notable expression of rage came in Ferguson, Missouri, in 2014, when the community exploded in response to what was perceived to be injustice in the acquittal of the police officer on trial for the alleged murder of Michael Brown.

Demonstration of anger continue to rock the country. Donald Trump's campaign speeches (2016) are repeatedly disrupted by violent physical battles, angry yelling in an attempt to make his speeches not able to be heard, and clashes between demonstrators and police. The character of democracy is supposed to be the proliferation and tolerance of different ideas, for the good of all, not the silencing of all who disagree. Anger has become the new wave of "How I get things to go in my direction."

America is traditionally said to be a melting pot, but lately it's more like a pressure cooker, just waiting to blow. We are all aware of the religious activity of ISIS sympathizers, the seemingly senseless random shootings in a wide variety of public settings, the hate speeches of Westboro Baptist Church activists, and even the progressively aggressive action of atheists against any expression of religion in the public forum. It's as if our country is sitting on a hot plate, rising in temperature, and percolating a rage that will one day detonate to widespread destruction.

Anger is a Window

Pastor Doug Bozung says, "Our anger is a window into what we really value, what is closest to our hearts." If that's the case, then what seems closest to our hearts is nonracist justice, religious purity, and political reason. But we are wrong to think America is so noble of mind. Comedienne Joan Rivers once said, "Anger is a symptom, a way of cloaking and expressing feelings too awful to experience directly—hurt, bitterness, grief and, most of all, fear." Possibly our national anger is not motivated by noble principles but by a self-oriented sense of vulnerability, and a fear that society is not going in the direction I wanted it to go in. In the movie "Batman Begins" (Warner Brothers,

© 2005), the character Henri Ducard says, "Your anger gives you great power; but if you let it, it will destroy you." Harville Hendricks, psychologist and counselor, agrees: "Pour a pool on the ground and light a match, and you have a raging fire. But put it in an engine, and apply the right spark at the right time, and the engine springs to life."[42]

I believe that the anger we see in America is expressing a frustration with disequilibrium. People have a deep sense that things are not as they should be, that something is desperately wrong. An atheist once said to me, "Now, after 20 years of being vocal about the positives of Christian faith, I would like to take some time to be equally vocal about the negatives I have found. i.e., Christianity and its controlling dictatorship, its historic blood trail, its plagiarized Bible stories, characters and concepts, the many human errors of the Bible and its contradictions, the brutal nature of its God, its involvement in the slave trade, the crusades, the inquisition, the witch hunts, its second-class view of women, its masculinization of God, its emasculation of men, its financial corruption ... you get the drift."[43]

Things don't "fit" the way people think they should, and they feel they are expressing a righteous anger about the disconnect they sense. Ironically, that perspective betrays that they have a concept of an ideal to which life should conform.

While sometimes anger is the response of a righteous heart against injustice, in this case it is a fire of discontent, raging against emptiness and meaninglessness. We are frustrated with politics, business, education, church, finances, and even trends. As far as the Church, "many of the 'nones' and 'dones' (those who are fed up with institutionalized religion) are demoralized by compromising reactions, if not outright denials, toward evil

---

[42] Harville Hendricks, Getting the Love You Want pp. 177-178

[43] U.K. rapper Jahaziel

in the church. … There needs to be greater moral courage to do the right thing, even if it costs you."[44]

A Christian Response

How should Christians respond to this new paradigm of angry activism? How much truth is there to the position? Despite that the anger is helping America wake up to some desperate wrongs, it fails on many points, the most obvious one of which is that their sense of disequilibrium is a false response. If they are weighing the shortcomings of our era by an assumed ideal, then an ideal beyond humanity and common to it must exist. And if that ideal exists, it must have a moral source. But these are the same people (the nones, the dones, and atheists, and the scientific naturalists) who deny the existence of God and a moral ideal. How can we justifiably appeal to an underwriting ideal and at the same time deny the possibility of an underwriting ideal? By definition, the very foundation of the template is self-defeating.

In Matthew 26.52, Jesus said, "All who draw the sword will die by the sword." Violence breeds more violence, and eventually those who perpetrate violence will also be the victims of it. Violence is to be seen in terms of all that violates a human being as he or she is before God and as they are in themselves. Violence is not another person's problem. It is everyone's problem. God called us instead to be agents of reconciliation. We are to become weak to win the weak, so that by all possible means we might save some (1 Cor. 9.22). We are to be priests, proclaiming the gospel of God that others might become an acceptable offering to God (Rom. 15.16). We are to be people

---

[44] Sarah Sumner, interviewed by Corcase Cheng-Tozun in "Righteous Anger for Jesus," *Christianity Today,* December 2015, p. 72

who show the patience of redeeming grace. The goal is to bring people into the Kingdom of God by every godly means necessary, not to usher people into the kingdom by arranging the meeting between a man and his Maker. The task before us is not to purge society of all godlessness by killing those who refuse to subscribe to our Prince of Peace, but to urge all society to repent from their godlessness and to love the Lord their God.

For too long Christians have been content to be part of the status quo, which has a mixed history of both progress and oppression. Power and money are corrupting influences, and we have gotten lazy in allowing abuses to perpetuate, as well as being involved in them. Instead, we are commissioned to be countercultural agents of justice and economic fairness, both of which are difficult stands to take in a culture driven by greed and the combination of money with power and success. We have contributed to the anger of Americans by casually living by the standards of the world instead of the standards of the Word. No wonder the Church is perceived as complicit in the demise of integrity in our country. We need to repent of our sins, conform to the principles of a just and moral society (even if it reduces the bottom line), work towards righteousness in business, politics, and education, and to create a new paradigm of righteousness even in the church. The Church has strayed enough off of the path that we are perceived negatively, when instead we should be living out 1 Peter 2.15: "For it is God's will that by doing good you should silence the ignorant talk of foolish men."

Summary

Many in our culture are expressing desperation and frustration in the form of anger, because life is too imbalanced, unfair, difficult, and meaningless to accept calmly. There is a widespread sense that something is wrong. Christians know that what is wrong is sin, and that our only truly worthy ideals have to be rooted in the character and nature of God, and we must live as agents of reconciliation and peace in a world plagued by horror, depression, anger, and waywardness.

Discussion Questions

1. Is there anything Christians are doing that is helping to fuel the culture of anger in America?
2. Why were thousands responding to the salvation message in cities, and yet the cities remain much the same?
3. It has been argued that the problem is not guns, but the souls and minds of those that hold them. Are there possible and reasonable public policies that can transform souls and minds? If so, what are they? If not, what is the Church specifically doing to fill the gap?
4. If what the Church is doing by way of training and ministry is not reducing the numbers of gun tragedies in our country, what paradigm changes are warranted in the church to bring transformation to our grieving world?

10

||||||||||||||||||||||||||||||||||||||||||||||||||||||||||||||||||||||||||||||||||||||||||||||

REALITY SHOWS:
THE NEW DECEIT

While reality shows have been part of broadcasting in America since 1948,[45] they erupted into mass popularity in the late 1990s with Big Brother, then Survivor, and a seemingly endless string of follow-ups. Americans watched in wonder as we could stare into people's living rooms, watch them on dates, and hear them compete to be a superstar of song or dance. Our pleasure was shattered, though, when other reality shows explained to us that some of the "reality" shows weren't reality shows at all, but previously arranged, somewhat scripted, and heavily edited. We were disappointed that our voyeurism was at least a little bit fake, and just another "gotcha" of TV advertising. Nonetheless, Americans continue to eat up the shows with hungry eyes and ravenous media appetites. "Who cares if it's fake, I want to see which bachelor she picks."

---

[45] "Candid Camera", first on ABC, then NBC, and finally on CBS

Alongside of that reality, with the expansion of the Internet we have learned to shop online and have become somewhat dependent on customer reviews to tell us about products we can't actually see and examine before we purchase. Again, it wasn't too long before we were all informed that companies were planting their own customer reviews in the mix to raise their ratings, give false impressions of their products, and generate sales based on deceit. Should we have been surprised?

The Information Age of multimedia and "knowledge by Internet" has foisted on us (by our choice, mind you) a paradigm of deceit. My niece coined a word that I have found to be applicable in many situations: deceiviant. Under the guise of authenticity, hypocrisy and deceit have become standard practices and prominent icons of American culture. We lie, and expect to be lied to, all the while valuing honesty and authenticity, with a wink in our eyes. While our culture preaches genuineness, and expects such from our political, business, and religious leaders, right under that pretty Formica façade, the wood is rotten. And yet we are repeatedly told that the millennial generation values authenticity above many other values, and they are angered by the hypocrisy they perceive in churches, politicians, and businesses.

> "Why do 'good Christians' think they can s*** on everyone else? If you're not white, too bad. If you're handicapped, Muslim, single, gay, or poor, f*** you."[46]

> "I am angered by the lack of true holiness in Christians."[47]

---

[46] TiredOwl, on reddit

[47] Finder10, on reddit

"Christianity is bleeding because very few young people want to be associated with an institution that is firmly associated with, and in a lot of cases teaches, bigotry and hate."[48]

"The self-proclaimed 'Christians' I had previously dated wore their wholesome masks well until **** hit the fan and then all of their darkness made itself apparent."[49]

"In my experience, church people are the least intentional with relationships, at least once you get established in the congregation. They bend over backwards for new people, but once you're in, they forget about you. At least that's what happened to us."[50]

They long for authenticity, and failed to find it in their churches. Non-belief felt more genuine and attainable. Sincerity doesn't trump truth, but it's indispensable, even irresistible, to any truth we wish others to believe. There is something very appealing about a life lived with conviction. Said one, "Christianity is something that if you really believed it, it would change your life and you would want to change [the lives] of others. I haven't seen too much of that." Churches, detractors say, just offer superficial answers to life's most difficult questions. The mission and message of their churches was vague: Social justice, and be good. The atheists seldom saw the relationship

---

[48] Birthday Cookie, on reddit

[49] denszil, on reddit

[50] Awards_from_Army, on reddit

between that message, Jesus, and the Bible. They didn't see the connection that the church doesn't exist simply to address social ills, but to proclaim the teachings of its founder, Jesus, and their relevance to the world.

A Christian Response

How should Christians respond to this paradigm of authentic deceit (or deceitful authenticity)? How much truth is there to the position? Despite the yearning for genuineness, the paradigm fails on many points, the most obvious one of which is this: Truth founded on deceit is meaningless and self-contradictory. By definition, the very foundation of the template is self-defeating.

By the accusations listed above, it's obvious that the Church herself has not conquered the false honesty of hypocrisy, which was probably the most rebuked personal characteristic by Jesus. This is a high priority if Christians want to make a serious impact on the unbelievers around us. Chuck Colson said, "God is dead not because he doesn't exist, but because we live, play, procreate, govern, and die as though he doesn't."[51] I don't have to pontificate on hypocrisy, since we all know quite well what it is. Instead, every person who claims to be a follower of Christ needs to cease and desist from any false representation. As Brennan Manning said, "The single greatest cause of atheism in the world today is Christians who acknowledge Jesus with their lips, then walk out the door and deny Him by their lifestyles. That is what an unbelieving world simply finds unbelievable."

---

[51] Chuck Colson, Kingdoms in Conflict (New York, NY: William Morrow and Co.; Grand Rapids, MI: Zondervan, 1987) p. 181

Summary

Our society acts with a mask of authenticity, but with a core of deceit. It's almost as if everyone knows there is no foundation to the building, but we continue to build anyway, because we all think it will never collapse. It is often accused that the Church is no different. Christians need now, more than ever, to separate ourselves from the lies of culture, be done with the hypocrisy that plagues our ranks, and live separate lives of integrity and truth.

Discussion Questions

1. Do Christians hide behind masks of their own? What might some of those be?
2. How can we reduce the incidence of hypocrisy in the church and on the part of Christians?
3. What can be changed about Church paradigms to express more authenticity from both Christian individuals and the Church in its practice?

11

||||||||||||||||||||||||||||||||||||||||||||||||||||||||||||||||||||||||||||||||||||||||||

UNBELIEF IN AMERICA: THE FIRES OF DISCONTENT

Atheism is growing in America. A Pew religious poll conducted in 2014 concluded that atheists made up 3.1% of the U.S. population[52]—double that of just a few years ago. Those who categorize themselves as religiously unaffiliated (the "nones") now make up 23%—a stark increase—of the U.S. population.[53]

People make a mistake to think that most atheists don't believe in God (though that is the case for the most radical atheists). Most atheists are more appropriately understood as atheist agnostics—they don't believe there's enough evidence for God to warrant belief in Him. They don't know if there is a God or not, but until verifiable scientific evidence proves there is one, they will withhold their affirmation in the existence of

---

[52] http://www.pewresearch.org/fact-tank/2015/11/05/7-facts-about-atheists/

[53] http://www.pewresearch.org/fact-tank/2015/05/13/a-closer-look-at-americas-rapidly-growing-religious-nones/

God. In other words, "guilty until proved innocent," or, in this case, false until proved true. Many atheists are ready to believe in God, if there were only some concrete confirmation.

This lengthy letter I received from an atheist shows what I mean. As you read, try to ward off your own thoughts assessing his words, and try to feel his pain and understand his perspective.

I am furious at the concept of God. If God is a person, then I hate Him. The @&$* fool resembles NOTHING of a personal God. He is NOWHERE to be found. This is becoming more apparent to me than ever, and I am finally able to see theologians for what they really are: deceived. Screw the problem of evil in the world. A much simpler soteriological problem is at issue here—and God, the blithering non-existence baffoon, can't do a d***** thing about it! I think I may pass out from anger. Unless you can actually calm this storm, this nearly uncontrollable rage and knife-cutting agony, please do not write back. I am in too much pain right now to take anymore from God, or worse, His people.

You Christians talk about "a personal relationship with Jesus." That's bulls***! You're all the most deceived people I've EVER come across! Idiotic, pathetic, stupid. How can I take you seriously?

The bottom line for me is that God is not a reality—EVEN WHEN I WANT HIM TO BE. So, $&#% off, please. (Sorry). I'm tired of your bull***, and the bull*** of all other Christians. God is supposed to be more than seemingly nothing. But, if God doesn't actually exist, how would you know in your blind faith that you're defending an idea that doesn't have a reality?

Frankly, I don't care about historical evidence of God, miracles accounts, etc. All that means NOTHING if God doesn't reveal Himself to a person. Think deeply on that. I know Christians will explain away what I'm about to say, but please hear me out. I want more than anything for God to be personal—to relate to me like He did with Adam and Eve in the garden, or like He did with Abram or Moses. But, if He doesn't do that, and if I'm left with just an ancient text and an idiosyncratic band of followers, I would be tempted to @&$*%*# just end my life if atheism weren't an attractive option.

You must realize this—AND PLEASE @&"$(*$& LISTEN (!)—Christianity has been nothing to me but heartache and absolute misery. I yearned for a God who never showed up (at least, apparently). I cannot be a "Christian" without #&%*#&$ losing my mind. And, if you can't understand that, then you're cruel, and NOT a blessing to me at all. A world in which God exists is a world in which I'd commit suicide. But thankfully, it is much easier to cope with life thinking He doesn't exist. You may secretly deep down despise me for making this choice, and may even act on that by threatening me with my eternal destiny like some know-it-all Southern Baptist/fundamentalist preacher. Well, I've got to say that, if you're wrong about God, you have wasted the majority of the only life you'll have before "lights out." But, you're not strong or smart enough to entertain that possibility with any level of seriousness, because, once you do, you know very well you will start to backslide. Best to maintain your defense mechanisms.

Do you know your religion makes me want to brutally @&$*%# murder myself? Like I said, that's why I don't hold to it. It's nothing but misery, and slavery. In short, I want a personal relationship with God, and that ain't happening.

In my experience and conversations I have found that people so desperately want a relationship with God, but so many just can't find Him. They are interested in spiritual things, "if only God would show up." I once asked a group of atheists why the arguments for the existence of God fail. I was told:

- There is no positive evidence for the existence of God.
- Lots of failed tests, too many. God is a no-show.
- Christians have a strong resistance to falsification of the hypothesis. Even when we can prove God is a no-show, Christians make up some excuse for His non-activity and non-responsiveness.
- There are no shortage of excuses to dismiss experimental results that don't fit with the hypothesis (Christians can justify anything).
- Very strong violation of Occam's razor (the concept that the simplest explanation is most likely the correct one).
- Christians with very little knowledge of or experience in science come up with the least scientifically sound explanations.
- Christians reference undetectable sources and unprovable means to explain phenomena.

- Christianity (theism) doesn't fit the data tightly (or even really at all: if you knew nothing of the history of the world but believed the standard theistic proposition that an all powerful, all loving god exists and cares about humans... well, let's just say you wouldn't expect the world to be anything like it actually is. Your model would take a strong hit based on how poorly it fits the data).

It's not that they don't want to believe in God, but that they don't see him, that God can't be proved, doesn't even respond to the prayers of his people, and doesn't fit the scientific data we have available. And until He does, there is no reason to believe in Him.

We have arrived to the point where one in five Americans say religion does not play an important role in their lives,[54] the highest percentage since the poll began asking participants about their focus on faith in 1997.

Twenty-one percent of respondents said that religion is "not that important" to their lives, compared to 16 percent who said the same in 1999. In 1997, 14 percent of Americans said religion did not play an important role in their lives. The increase is notably dramatic.

The poll showed that these less-religious Americans are more likely to be men, have an income over $75,000, to live in the Northeast or West and to be under the age of 35.

More than half of Americans still place a major emphasis on their faith, though. Thirteen percent of respondents in the new poll said that religion is the most important aspect of their lives, and 41% said it is "very important."

So what is the nature of unbelief in America?

---

[54] from a 2014 NBC/WSJ journal poll: http://www.nbcnews.com/politics/politics-news/losing-faith-21-percent-say-religion-not-important-n51256

1. Atheists think Christians are deluded because they live by faith over evidence.

This accusation comes to Christians in many different forms, but basically it's the thought that Christians ignore obvious truth and common sense for some sham of blind faith that motivates Christians to close their eyes, close their minds and believe obvious lies in the face of contrary evidence.

An atheist once wrote to me, "Christians are ignorant; they don't have the sense God gave a screwdriver. They believe in prayer over medicine, in fairy tales making ridiculous claims, and use God as an excuse for inaction and unaccountability. All they can say is 'God is in control.'"

Another wrote to me: Belief is so deeply valued by Christians, even over and above truth-seeking. Christians are taught to justify reality instead of discover it. So, he continued (as if we had to choose one or the other): "What do you value more: your belief in God, or an honest search for truth?"

They believe that asking Christians to have faith is a game God plays instead of just making Himself obvious by word and by sight. One said to me: "When my daughter was born I loved her and nurtured her and wanted her to know that I was the one who would protect her above everything (including myself). Why would God create us and then have us rely on blind faith? It's like me having my daughter and dumping her on some random doorstep with a note that says 'You will only be happy if you find me. I know where you are but if you can't find me somewhere in the world you will suffer forever.' Why would anything create a situation like that? If God is real, what's to stop him from revealing himself to us all—I mean actually not through some exercise of faith? My daughter knows that I exist and I love her and I know that she exists and she loves me.

78

It's ultimate, optimum and unequivocal. No test required. Why make something that needs to be discovered, found or believed in when you can just be there?"

I have been told that Christians treat blind faith as having the same authority as knowledge, and that we value faith over logic. "Faith is wishful thinking, and nothing more. I've always considered faith to be intellectually dishonest and steeped in willful ignorance and gullibility." And by another: Christianity is the religion of closed minds. Your faith forbids you to question your beliefs."

At bottom, faith is obviously perceived as a lunatic's approach to life, and the atheists' discontent with that perception burns ridicule into their opinions of Christians as pure idiots. The problem is that Christians don't believe what these distortions of truth and the misperception of faith indict us with. Faith is none of the things they describe. It betrays a farcical caricature of Christian belief. No wonder they're angry. Somewhere along the way too many Christians have assured them that we are not a thinking or rational people, and that what we believe has little connection to reality. Our faith has been miscommunicated as a blind leap off a high cliff in a murky fog—that to be a Christian is to be intellectually imbecilic.

2. Atheists think the Bible has been proved to be fictional, and Christians are willfully intellectually dishonest.

From science to geography to history and archaeology, not to mention logic, atheists are convinced that the Bible has repeatedly been proved wrong.

- The early books of the Bible have absolutely no historical background. There is nothing trustworthy about them.
- As a means of communication, the Bible is severely flawed. It has been altered throughout its history, parts added, parts removed, parts simply changed. There is nothing reliable about it.
- The material in Genesis never happened, the Exodus never happened, the Conquest never happened, there is no evidence for Joseph, Moses, Joshua, Solomon, Daniel, and so many others. It's all mythical.
- "The Bible doesn't match up with reality, but 'because it's in the Bible, it's true.' That's so wrong."[55]
- The Biblical text has to be assessed as wrong just as a matter of logic.
- The Bible, when looked at objectively, has so many problems with it. It has so many inconsistencies and contradictions.
- The Bible stories qualify as exactly that—stories—rather than exact accounts of what happened.

Their point is that if the Bible isn't true, then Christianity doesn't work. Their perception of the Bible is that the real disciplines at our disposal—science and archaeology—have shown the Bible to be laughably fictional, and they shake their heads in absolute incredulity that allegedly "thinking" people can give it any regard. "When I read the Bible, I don't see much credibility there. At all. There are websites devoted to all the problems with the Bible. And the logic of the teaching eludes me. Parables really are the best way to confuse everyone. 40,000+ denominations. And as far as the historical evidence behind it all, I just don't see much evidence for any of it." Their conclusions

---

[55] throwaway2920384, on reddit

are that Christians are intellectually dishonest, willfully ignorant. It is widely believed that if the Bible is not corroborated by numerous extra-biblical sources, it's not true. Therefore, almost all of the Bible is made up.

"I look at the Bible today and see a jumbled mess cobbled together to document the history of a guy who led an apocalyptic death-cult a long time ago. It's a fascinating story but definitely not something I want to base my entire life on."[56]

Another atheist wrote to me and said "An all-knowing, all loving, all powerful god would have the ability to communicate with his creations if he wanted to. What kind of lame deity would use written communication in an uneducated part of the world, in ancient times, when he could have just used any technology that we have available? If God's so clever why doesn't he just make a YouTube channel/Facebook page/Twitter/Pinterest and tell us about himself? Has he not gotten around to "creating" Google glasses for everyone yet so we can see exactly where he is? We are more advanced now than your god ever dreamed of becoming, for the simple reason that the people who created him couldn't imagine the ways we have to communicate now."[57]

As is obvious, the disrespect for the Bible is huge, and there is no end to the discussion of which stories deserve the most scorn:

- Adam & Eve, the Garden of Eden. "Science has proved all this to be laughable."
- The talking snake
- The barbarous and immoral God of the flood
- The ridiculous claims of the Tower of Babel
- Unproven narratives of Joseph, Moses, and the Exodus
- The false information of the Conquest

---

[56] Itsreallycomplicated, on reddit

[57] bobiejean, on reddit

- The fairy tales known as miracles
- The legend of the resurrection

3. Atheists think God doesn't exist because he can't be proved scientifically.

I have spoken to this perspective earlier in the book, but it fits this section as well. They want to know why Christians believe in God when God is not subject to scientific research and verification.

I have been told, "I was raised Christian. Now an atheist. I considered myself to be an atheist at 25. I'm 31 now. I took a look at why I believed in God and found no evidence, but found bad reasonings and confirmation biases. I've asked many Christians why they believe in God without any evidence. They point to the Bible and end the conversation. Please, where is the evidence?"

Others want to be able to test God, as happened on Mt. Carmel between Elijah and the prophets of Baal. Without such proof, it is reasoned, how can we know? They are discontent with any such claims, especially religious ones (the existence of God, the theological interpretations of history in the Bible, and the miracles), because they are perceived as radically without foundation. God can't be seen, heard, or confirmed; he doesn't answer prayer, his "actions" could be attributed to many other causes (or even just dumb luck), so what makes you think such a being even exists?

One person said to me "There is no such thing as evidence for the existence of God. Becoming an atheist for me was like breaking out of prison," and another said, "It's impossible that anything supernatural exists, by its very definition. Supernatural equals 'outside of nature.' Can you give me a coherent explanation of how something can exist outside of nature?"

"There is no more validity to the suggestion of god's existence as an explanation for scientific observations than there is for the existence of a purple unicorn wrapped in cellophane as the same explanation. They are arbitrary and baseless."

It's easy to observe that their discontent lies in that God doesn't show up with irrefutable empirical evidence, not only acting in our lives once, but also courteously waiting for science to set up an experiment and then do it again in a controlled situation. If God is not testable, then he is not actual, so the reasoning goes.

4. Atheists don't like Christianity because it is perceived to be judgmental, hateful, and restrictive.

Christianity is often condemned as judgmental and hateful by people who judge it and hate it. One such detractor said, "Christianity is a religion of discriminators. Religion is just a way to control people."

In 2013 an inquirer on Reddit casually asked the atheist sub for "Symbols of Christianity." The repliers didn't pull any punches:

- A straightjacket made from a security blanket
- A cross drooping so far to the side it looks like a question mark
- Fools gold
- A cage made out of crosses
- Virtual reality headgear
- A mask and ear plugs
- A veil

- A rabbit hole
- A blind man with glasses on

It doesn't take a psychoanalyst to discern what they think of Christians and Christianity. Christians were previously perceived as judgmental, but the same-sex campaign of the last several years, and some Christians' rejection of same sex marriage on biblical grounds, has raised up even harsher judgment and hatred of all things Christian by the critical opposition. But since morality, in their way of thinking, comes from public opinion, Christians are the ultimate sinners.

- Who the @&*$# are you to tell people who they can get married to?
- Why do Christians, as a whole, treat homosexuality as though it is "the ultimate sin"? You act as though being gay is irreparable, as though God will never love them, won't ever love them, and should never love them.
- How can Christians condemn homosexuals, since they were born that way and can't help it?
- What's so wrong with homosexuality? It's just two people loving each other. Why is that so awful and evil?
- Why does it seem to be absolutely okay to eat shellfish such as oysters and shrimp, but not okay to be homosexual? Hypocrites!

Since we're on the subject, atheists also get very turned off by the restrictive stance Christians take in general that is seen as sheer idiocy, in addition to things that are just sheer idiocy.

- A pastor won't allow his atheist brother-in-law to donate a kidney to save his life because it would keep him out of heaven, as if atheism could be contracted through transplants.
- Taxpayer money is used to build a Noah's Ark park in Kentucky

- A cracker turns into a piece of Jesus.
- The Salvation Army claiming "Gay parents should be put to death."
- Atheist club gets permission to meet on school campus; Christians respond with death threats.
- Married pastor molests men referred to him for counseling; calls the encounters "blessings."
- A man states that Hurricane Sandy was God's punishment for globalization.
- Pedophile priest tells a distraught seven-year-old boy that he could get the boy's dead grandfather into heaven in exchange for (what else?) sex.
- "My family thinks that asking questions (and perhaps thinking in general) is based in sin and doubt."[58]

Often the de-converted express joy at having escaped the shackles of Christianity. "Christians are so unhappy. I was looking at [my Christian friend] and never noticed it before but there's a definite slump to his shoulders, his eyes look glazed and he's lacking in energy. When I think about it now, the more I realize that this is how the far majority of the Christians I know are. They come across as lifeless, lacking in energy, depressed, empty somehow as if the life has been taken out of them. I suppose I had never noticed it before because I was just like them. I just find it very sad, though. As a side note, someone close to me has remarked on how now that I have left Christianity, I seem to now radiate energy and my demeanor is different, more confident with a carefree attitude. This has occurred in just a couple of weeks. I wouldn't wish to go back now for the world. If I can look and feel like this in just two weeks, what am I going

---

[58] demigrrl95, on reddi

to look and feel like in a year? Five years? Ten years? Leaving Christianity is the best thing that's ever happened to me."[59]

5. The De-converted have left because they want to have fun

They turn away from Christianity to leave the guilt and regret behind, and so they can start to have fun, and by that they mean drinking, drugs, rock and roll, and primarily sex, sex, sex. They want to be able to do whatever they want, think whatever they want, and be whatever they want to be. They find Christianity to be a type of repressive enslavement, and once they are able to shake off the shackles (and lock their conscience in a closet), they start hooking up and "bottoms up" with wild abandon.

- "20 years ago I de-converted, and soon afterwards, I experimented with shrooms and LSD, and the positive 'religious' one-ness experience of drugs sealed the deal of never trusting my subjective experience as Real, but at the same time, was also a very positive experience, felt more spiritual and more real and genuine than any emotional spiritual Christian experience."[60]
- "It's a great freedom to have sex whenever and with whoever I want."[61]
- "The farther I get away from Christianity, the more I have a 'live and let live/whatever makes you happy' attitude."[62]

---

[59] Heliosuntrix, on reddit

[60] bamtadah, on reddit

[61] guesswhoitis, on reddit

[62] harloxie, on reddit

- "I have less shame and don't feel the pressure about doing sin and hurting myself, or god's feelings with it. I will never again follow this religion of grief."[63]
- "I can be myself without feeling guilty about it. I can actually think about things and be reasonable. I understand now that I am merely being thoughtful, inquisitive, and encompassing, not a 'thought sinner'. I can also enjoy the entertainment that I love, such as punk, rock, and indie music, TV shows like Game of Thrones, movies like Deadpool, and writers like Bukowski."[64]

A group of atheists was asked (in April, 2014), "What fills the empty hole that God used to fill?" They said (1) Science, because it's reliable, predictable, and true, unlike Christianity, and (2) freedom: There is no general action or activity that is always wrong. I am free to use my own judgment on a case-by-case basis. The lack of a 'plan of God' is very freeing. I can take my universe where I want it to go."

6. The de-converted have turned away from Christianity because of unanswered prayer and non-experience of God.

Unanswered prayer, and not understanding prayer, are like gasoline on the de-converteds' fire of discontent. It is one of the main reasons people walk away from God. They see the way prayers are answered (and not answered), and their evaluation is that the whole project is unfair and nonsensical. "I pray and nothing happens, or things just get worse." In one sense prayer

---

[63] Eightypercentnormal, on reddit

[64] retnuh82, on reddit

should work, if God is who he says he is, but if God is who he says he is, why should he listen to us? We hardly get anything right, and we often have such mixed motives. And since answers to prayer are often so subjective, Christians are often accused of "confirmation bias"—when Christians see what they want to see, they interpret that as a confirmation of the effectiveness of prayer, and when they don't see what they want to see, they justify it with nonsense about "God told me to wait." When it comes right down to it, "we have no idea whether God answers prayer, because you can never tell, objectively, whether what happened was answer to prayer or not. There are too many variables."

One ex-Christian said to me:

> "I used to be a Christian (well, maybe). I was so for three years. And, ALL that time I struggled implicitly with things like this, no matter how earnestly I tried to seek God. Christianity caused me to become neurotic to the point of despair, and eventually I just gave in to failure. I speak about the existential aspect of experiencing/knowing God, because that's what I've sought for so long. And, relying on a possibly true historical account won't give me the experience I long for.
>
> I hope you can understand why I'm so critical of religion. It doesn't help me! But, I still allow for the possibility that God may exist. My only hope is that, if He does, He will reveal Himself to me beyond the fragilities of religion. I'd be happy to reject the Bible and still believe in Christ—if He reveals Himself to me. (But, of course, you would object to this, since you have God figured out). I am more critical of believers than I am

of Christianity—although, I am of that too, to an extent.

Anyone can become desperate enough to see what they want to see (to 'seek and find'). Seeing God is no exception. You know what I think? I think the Bible is the refuge for Christians to ignore the fact that God's voice and God's presence are nowhere to be found. And, I am not even talking scientifically! I am simply talking about discerning another being! As far as I am concerned, we are all the @&$*% alone on this miserable planet. But, Christians will then say that they 'heard God' or 'have experienced God.' 'Experiencing God' doesn't happen. Experientially, there is no basis for believing that He exists. Experiencing God appears to be no more than a mind game. And, this is me pissed off at this jerk (God) for asking me (through the Bible) to give everything... for nothing. I mean, sure, theologians can tell me everything that I might gain. But, when the rubber meets the road, what really do I gain?"

Another person said, "I have never felt God or even heard a word from him to any satisfaction for me believing there is someone listening. I not once ever went into it without anything but praying and pleading for him to inspire me into believing in him. But it never came to be. Does this means God doesn't love me or want me to see him, or better yet is no one listening? I will not lie to myself and live on a hope that 'he hears me but just being quiet to mess with my head.' He knows exactly what I will take from every interaction and what he needs to convince me He is there. The day I get that will be the day I will worship.

Why would he withhold himself from me? These are questions I ask."

The questions are painfully honest and the discontent is real. The "absence" of God is felt very deeply. If God really loves us, and wants us more than anything to be in relationship with him, and is willing to go to any and every length to make that happen, then His absence and silence are brutal knives to the back of honest seekers. If God would just reveal himself to the seekers, answer prayer in meaningful ways, and help people who beg for Him when they are in need, the hurting millions would rush to His arms. But this is exactly where they feel such emptiness.

> "I believe a God exists, but I don't believe that he is good, or merciful or even wise or just. … I can't worship a god who orders genocide, calls for the murder of queer people and rewards rapists with marriage, who looks at women as automatically impure and defiled."[65]

> "I am finally free from a deranged god who punishes people for eternity because they do what they cannot avoid and they don't worship."[66]

> "Why can't God make mistakes and be moral just like the rest of us?"

> God is a brutal killer: Uzziah, Ananias and Sapphira, the flood, Onan, Korah, the Sabbath wood-gatherer, the Canaanites, David's baby, Pharaoh's son…etc etc forever.

---

[65] Exmango, on www.reddit.com

[66] Newliferh, on reddit

"The biggest plot hole: God is love but creates a system that condemns the majority of people to eternal torture."[67]

The bitterness is biting. They feel betrayed by a God who allegedly "will never leave you nor forsake you." They feel abandoned by a deity dedicated to love. They feel so alone in the universe that they have declared God to be an illusion of gullible people so desperate for a spiritual connection that they are willing to make up a God, shut their brains down, create emotional highs, and make up His actions in life, just to survive without going crazy in this God-forsaken rock we call Earth. The unbelieving and ex-believing people feel a bonfire of discontent for a god who is not there.

Conclusion

As a final critique of Christianity, this person wrote about Christians: "Your abilities to think and reason rationally, empirically, logically, and independently, are immediately in question (obviously). But also your motives, morals and intent are suspect. A great many theists 'befriend' me, hoping to convert me to their beliefs (motives), take their moral guidance from some presumed, unprovable, jealous, conditionally-merciful, 'super-being' (or worse, from a fallible, repressed human mouthpiece representing and 'interpreting' said super-being's intent) (morals), and most are awaiting a rapturous end-time/eternity, where the 'good' are rewarded and the 'bad' are damned to hellfire FOREVER (based on our behavior during this brief twinkling of mortal being), and worse you are actively rejoicing

---

[67] FireFarmer74, on reddit

and encouraging this holocaust (intent), and doing everything to tell your '(G)god' just how good and deserving you are, by denouncing, protesting, and/or stoning and beheading those who still think/believe differently than you, those you think aren't devout enough (by your definition), and those (collateral) people who just happen to be in the neighborhood when you take your 'righteous divine retribution.' "[68]

---

[68] Chung_my_wang, on reddit

12

||||||||||||||||||||||||||||||||||||||||||||||||||||||||||||||||||||||||||||||||||||

FIGHTING FIRE WITH FIRE

"But after me comes one who is more powerful
than I, whose sandals I am not worthy to carry. He
will baptize you with the Holy Spirit and fire."
Matthew 3.11

"Are you tired? Worn out? Burned out on religion?
Come to me. Get away with me and you'll recover
your life. I'll show you how to take a real rest. Walk
with me and work with me—watch how I do it.
Learn the unforced rhythms of grace. I won't lay
anything heavy or ill-fitting on you. Keep company
with me and you'll learn to live freely and lightly."
Matthew 11.28-30, The Message

Despite the assault, God is at work in our culture. The attack on some fronts is strong, and godlessness is making some legal headway, but the strength of the Church, particularly the evangelical congregations (according to the statistics), is still a powerful force for the Kingdom of God on earth. Lives are being changed. Nonetheless, if the Church doesn't make some radical paradigm changes to rise to confront the new atheism, the drain out the church's back door will only increase. Without a doubt God is the answer to this generation's quest, but the church is speaking a foreign language to a culture that has moved on.

What are they looking for?

If I had to identify the three biggest issues, I would say they are looking for authenticity, evidence, and compassion.

We have always known that hypocrisy spoils the gospel as sewage spoils the sauce, but now even more so. In an era of instant communication, Youtube, and Google searches, there is no such thing as secret sin. While secret sin on earth was always open scandal in heaven, now it's also the seed of scoffing on earth. An infraction in little Middletown plays on Google's first page in towering Metropolis and goes viral on Youtube. Christian failure is fodder for the fall-away of thousands of borderline believers. For a generation actively looking for excuses not to believe in Christ, we hand them a ticket for an easy out with every false step we take. Christianity is being betrayed by its own adherents. While we knew God was always watching, we now have to always assume our neighbor is also watching, with cameras and bloggers everywhere. Every step we take and every stroke we make on our computer keyboards is public information. Our churches, life groups, and study groups must also become integrity groups. We need to step up to the plate and live our faith honestly in front of a watching world. Now is the time—for such a time as this.

The hostile generation also wants evidence. It is no longer good enough to say, "I accept that by faith." While faith is part of Christianity, there are answers and there are reasons. As a parent, I could have just told my children, "Because I said so," but I knew there was a reason for my decision, so I gave the reason. The time is ripe to answer questions with facts and figures, evidence and logic, reason and science, experiences and testimony, as well as with faith statements. This generation will accept nothing less "just the facts, Ma'am," so we need to give it to them. The evidence is there, so there is no reason to hold back. Christianity is presuppositional, but it is also evidentiary—one of its great strengths. Christianity is a historical religion, not just a philosophical one. Since the history, science, archaeology, geography, and apologetic evidences are there, we need to train ourselves to be able to dialogue effectively and reasonably about what we know to be true.

The ex-Christians and deconverted have left the church not just for intellectual reasons, though, but also for emotional ones. Over and over they tell stories of having been burned by people at church, mistreated, ignored, lied to, abused, yelled at, and misinformed. Back in the day when there was a biblical foundation to society and a Christian base in our culture, such behaviors would more easily be worked through. Nowadays, when there is so much atheistic encouragement available on the Internet, far too many people (young adults in particular) are all too ready to walk, and just need a straw to break the camel's back. We dare not give them one. Yes, we're walking on eggshells, but "love one another" is our calling and our conviction. It's not rocket science, and it shouldn't be difficult for believers in Jesus and children of the Lord. They want honest answers, true compassion, service in the community, a listening ear, authenticity, reasoned intelligence about spiritual matters, and sincere love from all. As a child we used to sing a little song that went "Be careful little mouth what you say; there's a Father up above, and He's looking down in love." It's not like one single stumble will make the world turn away from Christ, but the rancid accumulation of too many blunders is creating a culture of apostasy and a mass exodus from the church.

What is needed from the church?

The era of casual sermonizing needs to come to an end. If we don't address the questions and needs of this era, we might as well close up shop. While we don't need to preach to the Mensa population, we do need to stretch people intellectually as well as spiritually at church. We need to preach on apologetic and theological topics, even at times addressing some philosophical issues. Believers need to be engaged intellectually as well as expositorily, with evidence from the real world, honesty about the questions of our culture, and addressing the almost weekly issues rising to confront our faith in the news. Let's talk about them from the pulpit and in our study groups. Young adults are leaving the church because we never talk about the real things, and we give such simplistic answers. We are beyond saying "it's a mystery that can't be known," and "we just accept it by faith." We are remiss to say, "The science doesn't matter." It does matter. Truth is truth in whatever arena it appears, and pursuit of the truth is a high priority for us. Truth in one discipline will not and cannot conflict with truth in another discipline, and we need to pursue the truth wherever it leads.

We also need to drive ourselves to make our sermons more practical. While it has never been our goal to be biblically impractical, "so heavenly minded we're no earthly good," we need to work harder at discerning the culture and analyzing the needs of not only our congregation but of the neighborhood around us. Renewed and continual efforts at community analyses, listening to the abrasive voice of our culture, and perceiving the felt needs of the people in our sphere of influence cannot help but to benefit the pointedness of our preaching.

The Church needs to speak in love and not in arrogance. Our unsaved neighbors will not accept railing from the pulpit, which is perceived both as judgmental and rude. We need to speak a language that is not only appropriate, but that will also be heard. This generation is highly tuned to relationships. Too many churches are based on a paradigm of performance, and the relationships that young adults need and long for are at times missing. Churches need to explore new paradigms to create dialogue instead of speeches, relationships instead of spectatorship, and authenticity over "because I said so." The authority of the Bible is not even recognized as valid by many wavering Christians, so we must speak honestly and in love, including other evidences and cultural cues if we are going to be heard.

We must also listen, and not just speak. We have greater impact on others by the way we listen than by the way we talk. Rachel Naomi Remen said, "The most basic and powerful way to connect to another person is to listen. Just listen. Perhaps the most important thing we ever give each other is our attention. . . . A loving silence often has far more power to heal and to connect than the most well-intentioned words." Listening is an act of humility as well as compassion. We speak loudly with an ear that listens in love and honesty.

The Church needs a large dose of humility. We have battled our own heresies, our own political drives, our own culture, and even our own congregations so long that we too often speak with a voice of power than of meekness, of aggression rather than of submission. There is so much din we have learned to yell, to fist pound our pulpits, to confront our congregations, and to complete with the megaphone of our noisy civilization. In the process we have forgotten our "inside voice," the soft and still voice of true authority. We've been so stirred up for so long we don't know how to speak with a normal voice. Now is the time to breathe deeply, reorient ourselves, and speak words of true and humble authority.

We need to use questions to great effectiveness, allowing other people to surface the truth for themselves. Often if we are listening well and asking honest questions, we will show up shallow worldviews for the inadequacies that they are. A little humble questioning goes a long way. Simple inquiries such as "What do you mean by that?", "How did you come to that conclusion?", and "Can you explain that to me?" often result in our learning the weakness of the position being proposed, allowing us to speak honestly about the advantages of Christianity in respectful dialogue.

What is needed from the home?

Deuteronomy 6 helps us understand that the continual lifestyle context of faith in loving and respectful family relationships is the ideal vehicle for the transmission of our Christianity. The goal is not so much to pass on information, but to share life. The old adage, "Discipleship is more caught than taught" will always be true. Make time to mentor your children. Christianity is as normal as breathing and eating in a Deuteronomy 6 home. Prayer together is normal, conversations about faith are regular, and love and godliness characterize the home where faith will be passed on.

Research shows that dads are somehow the key. My work in youth ministry for 35 years taught me an unexpected truth: if the dads are not firm in their faith, we almost always lost the kids by the middle of high school. Dads seem to be the ones from where the children get their concept of God—whatever the kids think of Dad is what they will think of God. Movements such as "Promise Keepers" tried to make the same point, that dads so often hold the keys to their kids' spiritual walk. For much of recent history, research has shown that moms are more spiritually minded than men, but there's no biblical or spiritual reason for that. If we are to combat the drain of young people and young families from the church, it's time for men to come alongside the women of our churches and "Rise Up, O Men of God." Fathers need to be just as involved in the training of children in the nurture and admonition of the Lord as the moms. We only get one chance with our children, and then they're grown up and out of the home.

But the Church has to help. The Church and the home are not in competition with each other, but in cooperation and cohesion. In ancient Israel, the community was the church and the home, but nowadays we have forces pulling us widely and hostilely apart, creating barriers of time and contempt. TV seems dedicated to teaching children how to be disrespectful to the parents, and kids are quick on the uptake. The culture has more time with our children than we as parents do, and certainly more than the church does. Only with a coordinated, concerted effort from the Home Team and the Church Team can we hope to bring our families and neighbors into a healthy relationship with Jesus.

Conclusion

Even a quick read of the Gospels, along with the book of Revelation, shows us that the battle of God vs. Satan is more like shooting fish in a bucket than a duel to the death. Jesus speaks and the demons flee. He touches and the body is healed. In Revelation, the Battle of Armageddon is over in a Word.

The paradigms of our culture are all self-defeating, and yet they are gaining ground. The Church is too quiet against the lies, and we have lost our voice because of too many past (and current) stupidities. We hear the anger and disappointment of our loved ones, both family and friends. We feel powerless against the incessant godless driving of American culture. We know about the flagrant push against Christ on our college campuses.

But we also know that we belong to a reality where knowledge doesn't come only from our brains and strength doesn't come from our bodies. The race is not to the swift or the battle to the strong, but to the true and the faithful. Our speed and strength are not limited by the rules of the world. Our God is an awesome God, and it's time for a revival. Pray big. Live large and walk in the newness of life. The fire of God burns bright like a city on a hill, and it can meet the aggression of a hostile culture. But God will meet them through us. Jesus said we will do greater things than he did. This is our time.